CW00673536

Couples Therapy Workbook

Building Trust, Intimacy, and Communication for Thriving Relationships

Table of Contents

Introduction

Although human beings are one of many kinds of social creatures on this planet, there are important ways in which our interactions differ from those who also inhabit the animal kingdom. People are complicated, and they possess an unprecedented level of self-awareness. As a result, their relationships with others are infinitely more complex and powerful than any other interaction in nature. The depths of communication that human beings are capable of are apparent even in mundane, everyday relationships in daily life. Relationships become much deeper in friendship, but family and romance are where the power of human connection truly comes into its own.

As important and indispensable as romantic relationships are in any fulfilling life, they are not without difficulties. People in meaningful relationships bring all they have to the table, including their complexities. Long-term, intimate relationships are where all of these personal complications eventually come to the forefront, whether you like it or not. For these reasons, even the most worthwhile and fulfilling relationships can become difficult to maintain. Since every individual is unique, relationship difficulties can arise due to an endless array of reasons.

Even though every couple is its own story, luckily, there are many universally effective ways of strengthening and maintaining a relationship. If you're in a relationship that has entered a turbulent phase, know this is common. Most relationships will encounter problems at some point. Still, these issues can and should be resolved because preserving a valuable relationship is a worthwhile struggle. Whatever the crisis, the chances are good that you and your significant other can work through it and come out of these trials with an even stronger bond.

This book will help you and your partner navigate any tumultuous period regardless of your personal situation, character, the duration of your relationship, or any other specifics particular to your couple. Whether you've picked up this book to resolve ongoing problems or are just looking for information on how to improve and strengthen your relationship in general, you will find plenty of guidance and practical advice throughout the following sections. Of all the seemingly irrational aspects of the human experience, love is one that undoubtedly makes life worth living. Yet despite the frequent incomprehensibility of love, you'll find that many things you can do to cherish, nurture, and strengthen love are very practical and rational.

Section 1: It Starts with Trust

It's easy enough to say that love and passion drive romantic relationships. There's no doubt that these ingredients provide the initial spark that brings a couple together. Love and passion are also necessary to keep a long-term relationship going strong over the years. If these are the foundations of a romantic relationship, trust is the key building block that allows couples to continue raising their cathedral of love.

Building a healthy foundation starts with trust.
https://www.pexels.com/photo/man-and-woman-holding-hands-127120/

Love and trust, however, are quite different. Falling in love is a spontaneous force of nature; it flows out from deep within and is often inexplicable. It just happens and feels good, and people rarely have a reason to question such deep and sincere feelings. Trust, on the other hand, takes work. In the first section of this workbook, you will learn the nuances of what trust really is, why it's important, how it can be broken, and the steps you and your significant other can take to rebuild and foster trust.

What Trust Is and Why It Matters

While falling in love can happen with what seems like lightning speed, trust is built up gradually. Some people are naturally more trusting than others and can open up more easily, but building up trust always takes at least some time, even years, in some cases. Trust can grow naturally over that extended period, but building it can also be a conscious effort. Different people might have a million different ways of handling the issue of trust, but one universal truth is that meaningful relationships of all shapes and sizes require trust as an absolute necessity.

It's also true that focusing on trust is just as vital in trustful and functional couples as it is in those who struggle with it. Every relationship style will require both partners to show and justify some level of trust if it's going to work out. Couples that function well together, with partners who are open and sincere with each other, will always have to maintain that trust at a healthy level. Couples who have trust issues, whether they're a couple in therapy or are just having a minor turbulent phase, will have to do a lot of focused work to mend that specific problem.

Since relationships are all about emotional and physical intimacy, they require partners to open up to each other. Without opening up, it's impossible to allow someone to get to know you at a level that's needed for a fulfilling, long-term companionship. To open up to another person entails vulnerability. It requires you to break down your walls, forego your defensive posture, and truly let another person into your world. Most people have at least some natural aversions to such an idea because opening up in this way implies the risk of getting hurt somehow.

Trust occurs when you are able to do this with confidence and a firm belief that no harm will befall you. The essence of trust is feeling safe and comfortable when opening yourself up to your partner or spouse. In that regard, trust can be viewed as a key that unlocks the doors to some of the more sensitive parts of your life. These are the parts on which your partner will have to tread lightly if your relationship's bond is to develop to its full potential. While the aversion to vulnerability is common, most people can get past it spontaneously and without too much effort through the natural process of getting comfortable with someone. This is why folks with trust issues struggle in relationships; this problem can still be conquered.

The existence or lack of trust in a relationship is always strongly felt in any romantic endeavor, as there are numerous ways in which the level of trust manifests itself and shapes the relationship. In relationships built on trust, partners are more comfortable opening up and, as a result, give more to the relationship. When you trust someone, you'll have a much easier time forgiving them for simple shortcomings and mistakes. This allows you to work through problems healthily instead of always doubting your partner and expecting the worst of them.

Conflict is also much easier to deal with when people trust each other. Conflict resolution is all about communication, and this might sometimes require some uncomfortable conversations and the revealing of sensitive feelings and thoughts, which is impossible to do without trust. Navigating many common relationship problems necessitates giving one's partner the benefit of the doubt because human beings will make plenty of minor mistakes in their lives.

Shared interests, physical intimacy, and passion are some of the other things that bring couples together, but trust elevates their closeness and strengthens their bond on a whole new level. Couples built on trust are much closer and tend to know each other better. These feelings of safety and comfort with one's partner will infuse a romantic relationship with a profound friendship that works in unison with romance to create a lasting companionship.

Trusting couples are more self-sufficient because each partner will feel that there is hardly anything they can't discuss with their significant other. They rarely have to go outside of their relationship to seek support or advice. No topics will be off limits for them, which makes it possible to solve virtually any problem. Trust also makes it possible to be confident in all your decisions and plans with your partner. Words need to align with actions in relationships because this builds trust and provides stability, consistency, transparency, and respect.

If your relationship lacks trust, you and your significant other will feel its absence on many fronts. One common manifestation of mistrust is the erosion of personal boundaries. Relationships are about sharing a life with someone else, but healthy relationships always leave some personal space for each individual. Suppose you find it difficult to tolerate any boundaries your partner might like to establish. In that case, you're likely struggling to *trust them*. On the flip side, if your partner is overly invasive and overbearing, it's a clear sign that they have their own trust issues. There are couples where both of these scenarios are true, and an environment like this will almost always create a dysfunctional, toxic relationship.

Accusations, paranoia, and frequent arguments that arise as a result are also strong indicators that your relationship has a trust problem. As previously stated, mistrust makes it very difficult to open up, so there will be a lack of intimacy as a consequence. This can even translate into a lack of physical intimacy and impact the sexual aspect of your relationship. Relationships that lack trust are thus severely unfulfilling on both the emotional and physical fronts. Insecurity, feelings of betrayal, and fears of abandonment will also abound when trust is lacking.

The absence of trust can escalate small issues into misunderstandings and tension in the relationship.
https://www.pexels.com/photo/worried-couple-with-notebook-looking-at-each-other-4246239/

In summary, a relationship built on trust is one where partners or spouses can tell each other anything, ask difficult questions, enjoy occasional personal time without being questioned, and have a rich and fulfilling life of intimacy. This healthy state of affairs results in feelings of security, comfort, peace, and immense emotional fulfillment. It's also the kind of relationship where mistakes can be forgiven and misgivings understood. There is no fear, anxiety, loneliness, insecurity, or unconstructive arguing. Unfortunately, even a perfect relationship can enter a crisis period where trust diminishes. Trust should never be taken for granted and should instead be nurtured and kept from harm at all times.

The Many Enemies of Trust

Strong relationships between trusting and committed partners can weather any storm, and the trust in these relationships is naturally more resistant to challenges. However, it's also true that trust is beset on all sides by a million different curveballs that life can throw at people. These problems can often occur due to a person's previous life experiences that might have nothing to do with their current relationship. On the other hand, there are relationships where things that have damaged trust, such as past breaches of trust, need to be addressed.

Regarding past experiences, some people have just had bad luck with previous partners and, therefore, become insecure. For others, the issues begin in their childhood, which is a time when people are first acquainted with the basics of trust and are supposed to develop healthy attitudes toward it. Everyone begins their life with a natural need to rely on their parents, and the trust that a child feels toward their caregivers and is given in return plays a role in later development.

Excessive, overbearing control by untrusting parents or betrayals of a child's trust by the parents can be equally detrimental. This often leaves lifelong consequences and can cause people to always default to severe mistrust when they grow up. They struggle in relationships because they've never been taught in their formative years that trusting a loved one is a risk worth taking, with the reward being an emotionally fulfilling life. Witnessing mistrust between parents can also make a child grow up with trust issues, even if the child wasn't personally betrayed or treated with mistrust. While trust issues that stem from this source are particularly deeply etched into the mind, they can be resolved with enough dedicated work.

Unfortunately, people with a perfectly healthy upbringing and who are willing to open themselves up can also end up in relationships where trust declines. Even if both partners are like this, other things can happen during a relationship or before that relationship that will lead to mistrust. Betrayal in the current or previous relationship is one of the more common and obvious causes of trust issues. This usually happens through infidelity and can cause massive damage to years of built-up trust. It's not a deep-seated form of mistrust, however, as it's merely an incident that leads to fallout. So, trust can be rebuilt even after such an episode if there is enough will and effort.

Disagreements like clashing personal values or expectations can also damage trust, which happens when a couple has diverging outlooks on life, relationships, and other matters. Communication through meaningful, open conversations can help unite two people regardless of their differences, but it requires an open, non-judgmental environment.

Life experiences that don't relate to trust can also lead to trust issues in relationships. For example, people who have experienced a lot of social rejection can develop significant problems with opening up to others or trusting them. Frequent rejection leaves a lot of bad emotional residue, making people feel unworthy. People with this experience might find it difficult to believe that their partner's intentions are sincere, putting the very nature of the relationship into question. This problem can be exacerbated if a person feels they aren't getting enough validation or is neglected in the relationship.

These and many other problems can also manifest as jealousy, one of the most common obstacles in the way of trust. Jealousy is obvious, easy to identify, and unbearable, but it almost always has an underlying cause. For better or worse, many of these problems result from misunderstandings and communication barriers. This seemingly minor obstacle can cause so much pain, but fortunately, addressing how you communicate with your partner can fix many problems.

Healing, Building, and Nurturing Trust

Establishing trust is a two-way street. Sometimes, the problem is getting yourself to trust your partner, but in other instances, it's about getting your partner to trust you. Problematic relationships come in many forms, and trust isn't always the issue, but it does have to be maintained. Strengthening trust in a smooth, fulfilling relationship can also never hurt. Whatever your situation, the following steps can help smooth things out for you and your significant other in the trust department while strengthening your bond.

Identifying the Problem

Suppose you and your partner know intimately about each other and your lives before meeting. In that case, chances are good that you've already picked up on a few possible causes of mistrust between you while reading this section. Identifying the root of the problem is the first essential step toward addressing it. If you have a solid idea of the problem and are ready to take other steps, but if you just have a vague feeling of an overall lack of trust, you need to ask questions.

Continuous conversation is the key to healthy communication.
https://www.pexels.com/photo/a-couple-having-a-serious-conversation-5711600/

Conversation is vital, and different couples will have to ask different questions. If the trust issues stem from previous relationship experiences, then exploring those is a good idea. Be understanding and non-judgmental when doing this because digging around the past can bring all sorts of mistakes and grief to the surface.

Trust-Building Dialogue and the Power of Forgiveness

Engaging in all sorts of trust-building dialogue is how you identify the problem. Still, it's also how you devise a plan of action for you and your partner. One common starter is to discuss with your partner what trust means to both of you. While the definition of trust is universal, people can have significantly different perceptions. Talking about this will help clarify what each of you expects from the other. If you feel like the person who goes first might influence the other, it might be a good idea to write this down and then show it to each other at the same time.

If trust has been breached in the past, this also has to be discussed. It's one of the more difficult endeavors. Still, if you can have a non-judgmental, open-hearted conversation about these incidents, you and your partner will feel better and more confident in your relationship afterward. Reflective questions are also a great asset in conversations about trust. They will help you reflect on your thinking process and how you process certain things. How long have you been together? What was it that brought you together? What is the one thing you struggle with in your partner or yourself? What was it that hurt you the most? Engaging in guided discussions is often used in therapy, formulating a long list of pertinent questions to provoke deep reflection in the couple.

Forgiveness can be a difficult pill to swallow, but it's also severely underrated. If mistakes in your relationship require forgiveness to move forward, you should find it in your heart to make that step. As difficult as it can be, forgiveness is the key to fixing some relationships, and the question is whether you care enough to do it. If you reflect on this question, you will find that reading this book is a testament to the fact that you feel, deep inside, that your relationship is worth saving. If forgiveness is the only way to do that, you should try giving a second chance. The same applies to apologizing.

Commitment Letters

Dialogue is what will help you ascertain what the problems are and what should be done about them. After that, it's up to you and your partner to put those solutions into practice and reinforce your decisions. These solutions can sometimes require radical changes and significant commitments between partners.

To solidify your decisions and make it easier to get started, get your determinations out on paper, such as by writing commitment letters to each other. You and your partner can write down clearly and concisely what you will commit to in order to build trust. It would be a simple and straightforward proclamation that you will stick to.

You can give this a try below:

_____
_____
_____
_____
_____
_____
_____
_____

Trust Scenario Exercises and Regular Trust Check-ins

Great discoveries can be made if you and your partner develop a few fictional, trust-related scenarios to explore how you would think and act if they were to happen. For instance, if your partner has trust issues, you can present them with a hypothetical scenario where you are away on a business trip. Try to get your partner to open up and speak sincerely about what they would be feeling and thinking in that case. This will help you both to articulate the feelings and expectations related to trust in your relationship. Countless hypothetical scenarios can be invented for each specific couple, so it's a good idea to reflect on past arguments and situations where problems have occurred. This will help you develop the most relevant scenarios to explore and discuss.

After enough reflection and deliberation, you and your partner should have an idea of what you expect from each other, what the problem areas are, what trust means to each of you, and what kinds of changes in behavior and thinking you need to make to rebuild trust. It might be helpful to allocate a certain time each week to discuss your trust-related concerns while simultaneously commending your partner for what they did right that week. This would be a sort of debrief where you'd review the week and positively reinforce your trust-building plan. If you and your significant other have a detailed plan with many practical steps, it could be useful to create a weekly checklist of actions and then review each other's scores during the check-in.

Come up with trust-related scenarios and discuss them in depth.
https://www.pexels.com/photo/elderly-people-having-a-conversation-7117581/

Much of your efforts around trust will come down to healthy and meaningful communication. You will learn more about improving communication with your partner or spouse later in this book. Still, it suffices to say that relationships cannot be fixed if you don't talk openly and sincerely. Communication and trust are perhaps the central relationship aspects that permeate most efforts to improve other areas of your love life. Trust and communication will likely play a role in whatever you need to do to improve your love life, as you'll thoroughly learn throughout the rest of this book.

Section 2: How to Navigate Conflict

It's virtually impossible to be in an intimate relationship with someone without encountering at least some conflict. People have different outlooks, values, hopes, expectations, standards, and emotions. The clash of these factors among different people often happens even in mundane, daily relationships, let alone between people who spend years or an entire lifetime sharing their lives.

Conflict is bound to happen, and you must learn how to navigate it.
https://www.pexels.com/photo/couple-quarreling-in-kitchen-8560740/

As such, the difference between solid and dysfunctional relationships isn't that the former has no conflicts. The difference is in the destructiveness and frequency of those conflicts. If you accept that conflict is an inevitable part of the human experience, then the discussion focuses on navigating those conflicts with minimal damage. Navigating conflicts and reducing their negative impact on your relationship is a skill, and this chapter will aim to teach you that skill.

The Nature and Causes of Conflicts in Relationships

Once you understand that conflict is inevitable in long-term relationships and decide to learn how to handle it properly, the first thing to take to heart is that conflict shouldn't necessarily be feared. When you know how to process a conflict constructively, it becomes a fixable problem and might even present certain opportunities. Working around these issues inevitably improves communication and understanding. Getting through a conflict can strengthen a relationship, whether a marriage or anything else. Relationships fall apart not because of conflicts but because of what people do during those conflicts.

The trigger and true cause behind a conflict are two very different things. A trigger sets off a heated argument at a given moment. Still, the real reason conflicts happen is usually something underlying. People's personality types, communication styles, and personal stories will all play a role here, especially any personal issues associated with these factors. Extroversion and introversion, for instance, can produce their own conflicts. Introverted people might find it more difficult to open up, leading to frustration in their partner. On the other hand, extroverted people might not be as reflective as their partner would like them to be.

There are several personality type analysis systems out there that might offer further insights in this regard. For instance, the Myers-Briggs Type Indicator (MBTI) is a popular way of analyzing how 16 different personality types think and engage with the world around them. It's a straightforward questionnaire you can find online and fill out with your partner. MBTI isn't the most scientific analytical system out there, but there is no question that it has helped millions of people learn more about themselves. At the very least, it can provide a useful basis for you to start asking the right questions and reflect. The results could point you toward understanding more about why your personalities sometimes clash and where there might be room for compromise.

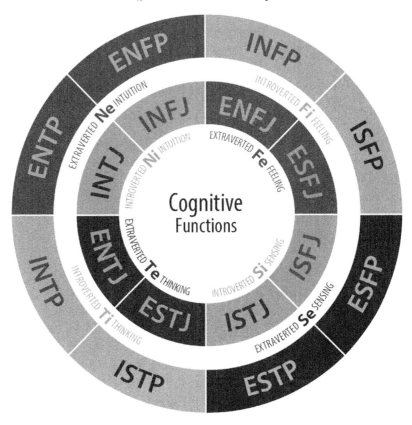

The Myers-Briggs Type Indicator (MBTI) is a popular way of analyzing how 16 different personality types think and engage with the world around them.
Jake Beech, CC0, via Wikimedia Commons
https://upload.wikimedia.org/wikipedia/commons/c/e6/CognitiveFunctions.png

Apart from personality types and communication styles, a range of personal and general life issues can arise and lead to conflict. Some common causes of conflict are those that don't necessarily originate in either of the partners. However, how people handle these problems can lead to conflict situations. Responsibilities around the home, money troubles, substance abuse, and problematic relatives can all infringe upon a relationship and cause tensions through no fault of the couple.

How the relationship is set up can also cause problems, such as if one partner feels too powerless and controlled or feels they're sacrificing and investing too much with no reciprocation from their partner or spouse. Some relationships can function on an uneven plain, but all people will require some kind of balance to feel comfortable. Poor communication, which is a problem in and of itself, can make these issues much worse. Partners can sometimes be unaware that they are too controlling or don't contribute enough because their significant other doesn't communicate their needs and expectations correctly.

Expectations can frequently become the epicenter of conflict in relationships. Most of the time, this happens either because one partner is making no effort to meet the other's expectations or because one of the partners has unrealistic expectations. The latter scenario will produce the same feelings in the unsatisfied partner as the former. This is because some find it difficult to differentiate between their unreasonable expectations and their partner putting in the effort. As always, this problem is solved through communication. One side needs to commit to doing their best while the other has to potentially adjust their expectations and ensure they're not smothering their partner with unrealistic standards.

Selfishness is another common pitfall in relationships. It can manifest in many ways, such as jealousy or neglect, but it's often an issue rooted in someone's background. Selfishness can lead a person to neglect their relationship and focus too much on things like work, but it can also cause one partner to require too much attention, leading to a lot of friction and dissatisfaction.

Conflicts can also crop up regularly due to quiet, built-up resentments. The irony is that such a sorry state of affairs can result from misguided attempts to avoid conflict at all costs. When your partner says or does something that offends or disappoints you, the best thing to do is talk about it honestly and openly. The urge to keep quiet to avoid an argument is completely understandable but leads to unresolved negative emotional residue. Not pointing these things out ensures that the problematic behaviors continue. Over time, the seed of resentment will develop, leading to conflicts much worse than a constructive discussion about your expectations and simple things that bother you in your relationship.

These are only a few examples of things that can go wrong, but relationship conflict has as many variables as human relationships. You can also apply a regular analytical approach to understanding the conflicts with your partner. For instance, you can keep a written record of your conflicts. This will make it easier to identify any patterns you might have missed or common triggers that lead to conflict with your significant other. This information is very helpful when trying to devise conflict resolution strategies.

You can try it by writing down the last conflict you remember in the space below. Try to pinpoint when and why it began, how it progressed, and how it ended. Conflicts often have a deep-seated, underlying cause, but it's a good starting point to at least identify the trigger and then take it from there. Analyzing the conflict with your partner can also lead to valuable, unexpected insight and feedback.

_____

_____

_____

_____

_____

_____

_____

_____

_____

_____

This is a good place to start, but if your relationship experiences frequent conflicts, you could perhaps dedicate a notebook or some other planner where you will write down the specifics of every conflict and maintain a permanent collection of such records. It can be useful to go back in time and compare notes to catch wind of any changes for better or worse. Either way, you'll want to keep previous incidents on record if you are to conduct a proper post-conflict analysis, especially when looking for patterns. It's important to stress that such notes should not be used as a 'gotcha' moment with your partner – but rather as a referencing method to avoid the same issues that plague your relationship.

In general, conflict in relationships mostly boils down to issues with communication. While it's inevitable and can happen for an endless range of reasons, the breakdown in communication makes conflict worse and ensures that its negative effects persist over time. As you can see in the above examples of the typical causes of conflict, a lack of communication is a common pattern of the problem, while healthy communication is the cure.

Self-Control and Understanding

The way you listen and communicate your concerns are two of the most important aspects of conflict resolution. When things get heated, try to stay level-headed while retaining respect for your partner and their point of view. To be more precise, conflict situations will require techniques for de-escalation to calm things down and minimize damage, as well as empathy to understand where your partner is coming from and what the conflict is about.

Communication Style Assessment

If you have frequent arguments with your partner, and especially if you've identified patterns during your post-conflict analysis, this can go a long way toward helping you get a better understanding of how you and your partner communicate. To manage conflict situations better, you'll want to thoroughly assess your and your partner's communication styles. Renowned American psychologist, professor, and therapist John Gottman provided valuable insights on this topic.

Gottman has devised the *Four Horsemen of the Apocalypse*. These four communication styles most frequently get in the way of constructive discussion and conflict resolution. Gottman's Four Horsemen include the following:

1. **Criticism** – Being overly critical toward one's partner in a very negative sense. Judgmental attitudes and character attacks.

2. **Contempt** – Treating one's partner with contempt, verbally or through non-verbal cues, demeaning them, and asserting superiority.

3. **Defensiveness** – Often manifested as a lack of willingness to assume responsibility for mistakes and instead pinning the blame on one's partner.

4. **Stonewalling** – Refusing to engage, giving the silent treatment, and generally shutting one's partner out.

In Gottman's research, a pattern of these communication styles effectively predicted divorces and breakups, assuming that the problems remain unaddressed. This is why engaging in the aforementioned post-conflict analysis is necessary, even if you must write it down. If you find that you or your partner engages in the above behaviors, you must address this together. Spotting these behaviors in someone else is easier than in yourself. Both of you need to reflect and ask yourselves whether you're contributing to conflict.

Below is a checklist of a few other ways the Four Horsemen can manifest during conflict. Next time you analyze a conflict, see how many of these you've exhibited, and ask your partner to do the same.

- Starting many sentences with "You."
- Accusations that your partner always or never does a particular thing.
- Attacks on the partner's character by pointing out flaws to insult, not to discuss the issue.
- Digging around the closet for past skeletons and grievances.
- Mocking.
- Sarcasm.
- Condescension.
- Assumptions, especially negative ones, about your partner's thoughts, intentions, feelings, or something similar.
- Aggressive, dismissive, or passively aggressive non-verbal cues like eye-rolling, forceful sighing, and scoffing.
- Any kind of insult, including name-calling.
- Saying things just to cause pain, especially things you don't mean. This usually causes regret later.
- Defaulting to excuses instead of evaluating and accepting personal responsibility.
- Never admitting any wrongs.
- Elaborate justifications of mistakes.
- Stressing the things you hate about your partner or even listing them.
- Cutting off the conversation
- Looking for an escape during arguments.
- Sweeping problems under the rug.
- Difficulty with articulating emotions or thoughts and expressing them.

Emotion Identification, Active Listening, and De-Escalation

When you and your partner are done analyzing a conflict and going through the above checklist, it's time for reflection and exploration. With a non-judgmental approach that puts criticisms aside, this can be an excellent activity for emotion identification. The first step is to consult with your partner by showing them which bits you've checked on the list and asking them if they agree that you did these things and vice versa.

This is a time for empathy, and it will help you identify many of the emotions at play during the conflict. When your partner says you've done a certain thing they dislike, don't immediately default to disagreeing with their assessment, even if you strongly feel that they're wrong. Instead, you want to engage in active listening, which means showing a genuine interest in their point of view, being empathetic, and respecting their thoughts.

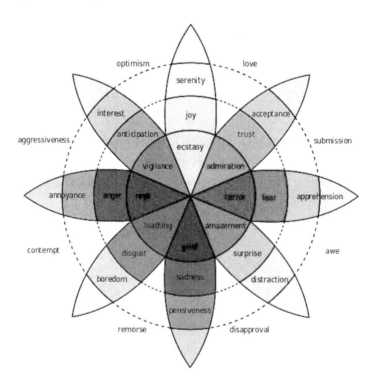

This emotion chart will help you identify many emotions that you may not be able to figure out at times.

Encourage them to divulge more of their perspective by using verbal and non-verbal cues to be as responsive as possible while you listen. If they lay out their case constructively and you still disagree with their assessment, perhaps you'll be able to identify some of the negative behaviors in their feedback. Active listening is about encouraging your partner to open up more and more. When they're done with a statement, you should ask them open-ended questions or try to summarize what they said to see if you understood them. This is how you get to the root of the emotional factors behind your issues. These conversations could also be a great addition to your conflict diary, next to your summaries and analyses of previous conflicts.

While the above exercises mostly involve understanding your conflicts and resolving them for the long term, keeping these things in mind should also assist with de-escalation in the heat of the moment. So, acquaint your partner with what you've learned here as soon as possible if you're having frequent conflicts. You can try to keep the communication style assessment checklist in mind and do the opposite of those behaviors next time you get into an argument.

A simple change in communication, such as opting to start your statements with "I" instead of an accusatory "You," can be surprisingly effective at calming things down. For instance, "You always make me feel worthless" has a much more hurtful connotation than "I feel like I deserve more respect from you." This is much more likely to elicit a positive and reflective response that leads to deep thoughts and introspection in your partner, especially if you are caught in a vicious cycle of conflict.

If the situation allows, conflicts can also be de-escalated through time-outs. If things get too heated, try going to another room for a few minutes to collect your thoughts and calm down. After that, you can come back and pick up where you left off, but now with a cooler head and perhaps a few good ideas on how to proceed. If you can do this, you and your partner already possess a substantial level of self-control you can build upon.

The Importance of Compromise

When things are back under control, and you start getting a handle on the problem, it's time for the finer touches. This means efforts to find common ground and negotiate, which is how conflicts are resolved in the long term. This is the way for you and your significant other to find real, sustainable solutions and reinforce the foundations of your relationship. It's how you find things to agree on and make steps toward minimizing conflict in the future.

Negotiations and Common Ground

To find common ground and identify which compromises can or must be made, you simply have to talk, perhaps more than ever. Finding common ground starts as a game of elimination. You and your partner should identify negotiable and non-negotiable things for you. That which is non-negotiable can then be eliminated and taken off the table. Personal values are a common example.

It's good to reflect together on some of the things you have in common that bring you closer, especially positive things. Starting with the fact that you both care about the relationship and each other is a valuable reminder that love exists between you. When you start on that path and go where it takes you, it quickly becomes clear that you have a lot of common ground.

From that point on, it's all about focusing on the problem you've identified through previous exercises and seeing what both of you can contribute to its resolution. Compromise means that both sides will give something to the cause in the interest of a higher goal. You both have to know what you need and want and listen attentively to each other.

In a joint effort, you and your partner should identify as many things you agree on as possible. You both want fewer arguments, which is a good foundation to build on. What is it that needs to change for you to get there? If you've successfully identified and thoroughly discussed the causes of your arguments, potential solutions should emerge. This is where negotiation comes into play because solutions entail changes and alternatives likely to impact you or your partner in some way.

Finding compromise in any relationship also has much to do with balancing personal and relationship needs. Relationship needs are required to keep your relationship going strong, and they are the needs that will often require some adjustments or sacrifices on the personal front. Compromise is how those sacrifices can be minimized. For example, a conflict might arise over a hobby that a spouse enjoys but spends a lot of personal time on. The other spouse will voice this concern in a way that doesn't just demand the cessation of said hobby but suggests adjustments. A compromise in this situation would be to take up that or some other hobby together or to adjust the schedule.

All of this should be enough to get a foot in the door and start gradually addressing the root causes of your conflicts while learning ways for your partner and yourself to handle yourselves better when conflict does arise. Don't be discouraged if you still struggle to communicate and practically apply what you've learned in this chapter. Later in the book, you will learn all about communication specifically.

Section 3: Increasing Intimacy

Since romantic relationships are all about sharing your life as completely as possible with another person, your ability to be close to each other without holding back is critical for the relationship's success. Knowing someone intimately and being very close emotionally occurs outside of romantic relationships, too. Familial relationships, or even those between close/lifelong friends, have their own kinds of intimacy.

The road to everlasting intimacy takes work in any relationship.

However, romance is where intimacy takes on its most evolved form, partly because love makes people more susceptible to being vulnerable. Still, there's also the question of physical intimacy. The intricacies of romantic relationships can lead to unusually complex interpersonal issues. So, these relationships require a special emphasis on intimacy. This is precisely because intimacy leads to openness, emotional comfort, security, and vulnerability.

All of these are prerequisites for truly sincere, healthy, open communication, allowing trust to flourish and resolving conflicts. Since intimacy is such a critical aspect of a fulfilling relationship, this chapter will look at some insights into how you and your partner can deepen and enhance your intimacy.

Intimacy in Romantic Relationships

Intimacy in romantic relationships occurs when you and your partner feel profoundly close to each other and have a deep connection. People with this level of intimacy between them also have an intimate knowledge of each other, which enables understanding and perhaps the highest manifestation of empathy that human beings are capable of. Intimacy is often associated with the sexual aspect of relationships and is sometimes mistakenly used as a synonym, but it's much more than that and comes in many forms. All of these forms are equally important. To properly understand how intimacy plays a part in a relationship, it's best to break it down into a few particularly common forms, specifically in romantic relationships.

Physical Intimacy

Physical intimacy in a relationship relates to a couple's sex life, of course, but it's also about much more than that. Couples who are in a functional, fulfilling relationship have their own physical language of gestures and contacts that reinforce the intimate nature of their relationship regarding their overall closeness, not just sex.

There exists a very natural need that we all have for physical touch, which is why even the most mundane physical contacts that have nothing to do with sexual intercourse will spark up your love hormones like oxytocin. Oxytocin is one of the reasons physical contact fosters a feeling of closeness, and it occurs not just in romantic relationships but also between parents and children and in other close relationships. Oxytocin is colloquially known as the love hormone but can also be seen as the connection hormone. Oxytocin leads to feelings of comfort, fulfillment, and calm between people who love each other. It is why humans enjoy cuddling, holding hands, massages, and other similar contact, in addition to sexual interactions.

Emotional Intimacy

Emotionally intimate couples find it easy to express themselves and open up because these are relationships where vulnerability is rewarding and carries no risk of being hurt. Emotional intimacy makes you feel validated and understood when you open up to reveal your innermost feelings and thoughts.

Many people learn emotional intimacy through a healthy upbringing, but it's never too late to improve it. Couples that lack emotional intimacy usually have a diminished sense of security and safety. Of course, trust plays a major part in this aspect of relationships. If you find that whenever you're in a state of distress, your first thought is to talk about it with your spouse or partner, that's a good sign that you are emotionally intimate with them.

Intellectual Intimacy

Intellectual intimacy makes partners relate to each other through shared interests, hobbies, and similar passions. It's also called mental intimacy because it's all about having an intimate understanding of how your partner thinks. This type of intimacy is common between people who share a bond in all types of relationships, not just romantic ones.

Still, romantic partners will always find that being intellectually intimate makes their bond stronger and more exciting. While being emotionally and physically intimate is crucial in all romantic relationships, some people find intellectual intimacy more important than others. It always helps make a relationship more interesting, so it can't hurt. Still, some will actually build their entire relationship around shared intellectual interests. This is because some individuals are naturally attracted to intelligence, and the idea of sharing everything that has to do with work, hobbies, activities, studies, and other similar pursuits with their partner is what they look for. Those who are attracted to intellectual intimacy in a partner are referred to as *sapiosexuals.*

Spiritual Intimacy

This form of intimacy is also somewhat broad, as it can relate to anything from religion to values, ethics, or overall life philosophy. Spiritual intimacy leads some people to believe they've found a "kindred spirit" or "soul mate" in their partner. Spiritual intimacy occurs in various settings and relationships, but it also does well in romantic relationships. If two romantic partners share similar beliefs, they will likely share quite a few things in their worldview and life outlook.

This kind of connection is valuable because it can help people in a relationship find common ground more easily, agreeing on the ways they want to live their lives and what to pursue. Couples find spiritual intimacy through religion, volunteering, reading, or more modern activities such as yoga. Some couples can function without always aligning their values and beliefs, but disagreements can lead to conflict.

Experiential Intimacy

As its name suggests, experiential intimacy is about a couple's experiences together. This kind of intimacy is quite easy to build up, as it only requires you and your partner to take up new activities together, which can be leisurely, work-related, or anything else. The important thing is to share those experiences.

Engaging in activities together builds upon the foundation of your relationship.
https://unsplash.com/photos/couple-sitting-on-edge-while-looking-at-the-mountains-vWqK0KsNTXQ

Engaging in activities you are both interested in is a great way to spend time, but new experiences can be an opportunity to grow closer to your partner. For instance, it's not uncommon for one partner to enjoy something the other partner knows almost nothing about. Joining your partner or having them join you for these experiences can teach you new things about your partner and life overall.

These are only a few of the ways in which intimacy manifests in relationships. The common theme among all these forms of intimacy is that they lead to a stronger bond and tend to have a pleasant, calming effect on you. When you feel truly comfortable and at peace when engaging in or talking about any of the aforementioned moments of intimacy, you know that you and your partner have a truly special bond.

Problems in the Way of Intimacy

At this point in the book, you can probably begin to see how many relationship problems and solutions to those problems tend to feed into each other. For instance, it's clear that a lack of communication will impact a couple's ability to be intimate the way they need to be. It can also be the other way around, with a gradual loss of intimacy leading to more conflict, distance, and an overall breakdown in communication.

Stress and Sex Life

While intimacy isn't all about sex, a loss of sexual intimacy is indeed one of the more common problems. One of the most frequent causes of problems in sexual and other forms of intimacy is stress. Stress can be related to the relationship itself. Still, it's also unfortunate that stress from other parts of your life can seep into your relationship or marriage and build walls where there were none before. People who are stressed out find it difficult to relax in most settings. Suppose you or your partner are feeling uncomfortable and constantly worrying in general. In that case, it's no surprise that it might also reflect on your relationship.

Stress is especially harmful to a couple's sex life because of its effects on the sex drive. Men are especially vulnerable to stress in this regard. More often than not, stressors in a person's life, such as problems at work or financial troubles, lead to chronic tension every day. The problem occurs when a person starts looking for ways to handle their stress and ends up going for solutions other than sex, such as sleeping or engaging in other activities.

A particularly troublesome complication in such a scenario is if the other partner interprets the lack of interest as an indication something is wrong with them. This can produce insecurity, friction, or even resentment. Spicing things up in the bedroom to increase interest can work sometimes, but it can also backfire. It's best to focus on the true cause behind the stress and tackle it directly instead of just wrestling with the symptoms. Suppose you or your significant other is struggling with something in or outside your relationship. In that case, you must talk about it and help each other shake off that burden. Otherwise, walls might start building up between you.

Obstacles to Overall Intimacy

Speaking of walls, a lack of communication can ruin a relationship's intimacy more thoroughly than miscommunication and conflicts. Despite its potential destructiveness, the conflict will at least raise some passion. In some cases, negative communication can be better than no communication. When partners shut each other out, become unresponsive, and stop sharing their problems, little can be done to increase intimacy before reigniting communication.

If there are frequent arguments, those should be addressed in the ways discussed earlier. If there is no communication at all, something has to be done to get it flowing again, even if it initially leads to tensions. Getting communication going from scratch might sound daunting, but a lot can be done, as you'll learn later in this book.

Busy schedules are another interfering factor that can chip away at your relationship over time. Work and children tend to be the primary factors that make couples too busy to spend quality time with each other. If you've had this experience and suspect it has infringed upon the intimacy between you and your partner or spouse, it's an issue you must address. When work and children work in unison to fill up your schedule, there is no shame in seeking help regarding child care, for example. Paying a babysitter or asking a relative to watch the kids at least once a week so you can enjoy some quality alone time can do wonders.

Get a babysitter to allow you to have quality time together without the kids.
https://www.pexels.com/photo/a-woman-story-telling-with-two-children-in-bed-6974717/

Perhaps the most elusive of all intimacy's enemies are *various personal issues*. These can be difficult to deal with when one of the partners won't share their problems, but even when they do, such issues can be severe and require lots of work. These include things like self-esteem problems, past trauma, a painful upbringing, personal tragedies, and a range of physical or mental health problems. Sometimes, seeking professional help to work through these troubles is necessary and should under no circumstance be regarded as shameful.

Strengthening and Nurturing Intimacy

Once you understand intimacy and its enemies, it'll be easier to determine whether your relationship is lacking in that department. If improving and maintaining a satisfying level of romantic intimacy had to be boiled down to three main components, those would be communication, physical contact, and quality time spent together.

Defining Intimacy as an Exercise

A great place to start your journey toward reigniting the spark is to simply sit down with your partner and discuss intimacy. As a simple exercise, you can make an evening out of it. Over dinner or some other comfortable setting conducive to conversation, you could both take your turn trying to best define what intimacy really means for each of you.

As you've seen above, the basic definition of intimacy is straightforward enough, but there's still a lot about intimacy left to the individual's perception and expectations. The end goal is always to be closer to the person you love. Still, in pursuit of that goal, some people might put an emphasis on sex. In contrast, others might think deep conversations or shared new experiences are more important. Intimacy is a feeling, so you must think back and identify situations where you felt the most open, connected, and comfortable with your partner. Those will be the situations and interactions that probably mean the most to you regarding intimacy.

For instance, you and your partner can think up or write your own lists of all the things you feel would increase intimacy and should be added to your relationship. You can let your imagination run wild because the list can include realistic and unrealistic things. The key goal is to give your partner a better idea of how you perceive intimacy.

Sensual Exploration

As mentioned, the role of physical touch, both sexual and non-sexual, is vital to romance. Try to imagine a stereotypical happy couple and how they interact with each other. There are hundreds of non-verbal cues that couples use, mostly unconsciously, to express their affection. They constantly touch each other, teasing, scratching, caressing, leaning on each other, smooching, and much more. These things are really second nature for people who are in love and have a healthy intimacy level.

Physical touch is a major part of how human beings communicate with each other in all manner of relationships and interactions. It's about much more than sharing information, though. It's long been known that the amount of physical touch a baby gets from the mother affects how the child will develop. The role of non-sexual physical touch in romance has also been studied, and it has been shown that couples who casually touch each other all the time report feeling more satisfied and intimate in their relationships. Studies have confirmed what everyone could always see; however, observing a happy and unhappy couple sitting next to each other can really speak volumes.

While this stuff comes instinctively to most people, couples who have lost the spark can and should relearn it. Activities that will allow you and your significant other to engage in the basic sensual exploration of each other are plentiful. It can be as simple as having a movie night together in bed. You might have to remember to cuddle at first, but soon enough, you'll find that it happens on its own as intimacy grows.

Reinvigorating Intimacy through Activities

Hobbies and other activities will always boost a couple's experiential intimacy. Still, depending on the activity, this can simultaneously improve intimacy on many levels. You really can't go wrong with new hobbies that you and your partner find interesting and engaging. As long as it's a constructive, healthy activity, it can only help.

Remembering that date nights aren't just for newly formed couples is important. Most relationships start with regular dates, so returning to such simple activities can refresh a longtime relationship. It can be a nostalgic experience that brings up good old memories and excitement. A fancy dinner once a week is a good opportunity to unwind and foster communication, and a new outdoor activity could reinvigorate both of you mentally and physically.

A dinner date is a great way to switch things up and connect intimately away from your usual surroundings.

The options are endless, but the important thing is that you both enjoy these activities and feel comfortable with them. Sitting down and coming up with new, exciting ideas for all the things you could do together is an excellent and therapeutic exercise in and of itself. It'll encourage you both to open up about the things you want to do and experience, and it might even remind you of all those things about your partner that made you fall in love in the first place.

Make a Weekly Schedule

Some couples can easily jump into new activities with a degree of spontaneity, but a more structured approach could work better for others. Creating a schedule is particularly helpful for busy couples. As an exercise, you and your partner can sit down to discuss ideas for activities you'll enjoy. Afterward, you can run these against both of your weekly schedules to agree on a time that suits you.

You can use the template below to create a very simple weekly schedule, putting in a time for each day and a brief description of the activity you've got planned. It's normal if you aren't able to set aside time every single day of the week, so don't let that discourage you. Some days can be rounded off with a simple yet special dinner at home at the end of the day, accompanied by meaningful discussions. Remember, if you're working on problems like communication and engaging in exercises found throughout this book, those will also work as intimacy-building activities.

Monday:

Activity:

Tuesday:

Activity:

Wednesday:

Activity:

Thursday:

Activity:

Friday:

Activity:

Saturday:

Activity:

Sunday:

Activity:

Section 4: Master the Art of Communication

As you've seen in the previous sections, communication is a matter that comes up repeatedly regarding overcoming problems in a relationship. In essence, a relationship is a form of communication between two people, but it can attain a level of intimacy seldom seen in other forms of human relationships. In a way, a romantic relationship as a manifestation of communication is a special language; the only people who understand it are the two who share that special bond.

Communication is the answer to any tension that might be building up within the relationship.
https://www.pexels.com/photo/cheerful-multiracial-couple-looking-at-each-other-3776877/

When communication breaks down, and barriers are erected, the couple begins to lose that special understanding, and they eventually forget how to relate to each other the way they did before. No matter how strong the bond is between two people in love, communication must be nurtured and preserved. While you've already learned quite a few things about communication in relationships, this section will take a closer look at what communication should look like, what common issues it might face, and how to foster it with your significant other.

What Healthy Communication Looks Like

Suppose you see communication as the transfer of information and consider your relationship a system that relies on accurate, unfiltered, and comprehensible information. In that case, it's easy to understand the practical value of effective communication. Communication is the essence of any attempt to improve human relationships, and most other efforts will be in vain without it.

You must understand what healthy communication looks like if you are to define what problems you might have and which goal you'll be pursuing. If healthy communication had to be summed up with a single concept, that concept would be comfort. One of the first questions to reflect on is whether there are topics or concerns in your relationship that induce any level of anxiety when you think about discussing them with your partner. If you feel anything might be off limits for some reason or supposedly better left unsaid, you and your partner probably aren't communicating on the best frequency.

Comfort in communication exists when there's no question you're afraid to ask and no topic you are reluctant to bring up. When healthy communication is established, you will feel your partner is the one person you can lean on and expect to engage you with understanding, empathy, and patience. Not every topic is right, and some are not worthy of discussion, but that doesn't matter in a healthy relationship. Everything can be talked about, and all issues can be ironed out well before they develop into something worse.

In healthy communication styles, partners are on an equal footing. They don't speak over each other, interrupt, or demean what the other side is saying. They will take turns and constantly encourage each other with feedback, thus facilitating sharing. Both parties will maintain a degree of self-awareness, being mindful of their actions and how their behavior and mode of expression might affect the other side. As section two of this book describes, active listening is an integral part of this process.

Honesty and kindness are some of the clearest signs two people communicate properly. Being truthful in relationships is about much more than just telling the truth about relatively unimportant things. Never telling lies is very important, of course, but in intimate relationships, silence can be a lie in and of itself. The problems people ignore -and the important things they leave unsaid - can damage or completely destroy a relationship, regardless of how long it has been.

Getting over your anxiety to bring up certain things is one side of the coin. Still, the other is making sure that you don't do anything to cause the same problem in your partner. Sometimes, it can be difficult to determine whether another person is being open about their thoughts and feelings, but it's much easier to see these things in someone you know very well. Body language can be a major indicator of how comfortable someone feels during communication. Stable eye contact, open body postures, relaxed sitting, physical direction, and other similar cues are signs that someone is comfortable in an interaction.

How concerns are raised can also provide insight into the quality of communication between you and your partner. There is a big difference in results between raising concerns in a hostile, judgmental, or insulting manner and opening up the conversation with kindness and empathy. A common way to express concerns healthily is to intertwine the negatives with positive, reinforcing speech that reminds your partner that you appreciate them.

For instance, dysfunctional relationships see instances where people will just tell their partner that they hate a certain thing they do, focusing intensely on the negativity in the situation. On the other hand, a considerate, loving partner will tell their significant other that they love and respect them, outlining some of their virtues and positive qualities that they appreciate. Then, they will add the part that bothers them.

Clarity, active listening, empathy, and patience are the building blocks of healthy communication. People who communicate with ease are kind, succinct, and easy to understand. These couples have no problem getting to the point of the matter, and they are able to do so without emotional damage and friction, even when dealing with the most difficult topics.

Common Pitfalls

Something to focus on is the balance between speaking and listening. Suppose you often give prolonged monologs or rants without meaningful feedback. In that case, your partner isn't participating in the conversation on the level they should be. Conversely, suppose you're always playing the listener and can't get a word in. In that case, you're the one who isn't getting the opportunity to express yourself. Both of these imbalances can occur due to either the speaker's aggressiveness or the listener's excessive passivity.

Another common cause of communication problems is the reality of substance abuse and addiction in general. Typical symptoms associated with addiction include a lot of behaviors that make it difficult to communicate sincerely and openly. People who struggle with these issues are often dishonest and refuse to accept responsibility for their mistakes. They also tend to be extremely defensive, deflective, anxious, aggressive, and outright abusive.

On a positive note, addiction and substance abuse are easy to identify, so it's not difficult to determine what must be done. The trouble is that the problem can be rough in some cases. If you and your partner are dealing with these issues, seek out professional help or the assistance of family members. As always, though, it has to start with communication. If your partner is the one with a problem, the first step is to get through to them and convince them that the problem is real and requires solutions.

Whether you do this alone or with someone else's counsel, one of the more effective strategies is to convince your partner that what they are doing is destroying your relationship. Unfortunately, extreme cases might require you to give them an ultimatum, but this can backfire if it's done with judgment and hostility. Instead, their wake-up call needs to be rooted in the love and understanding for you (as their partner) and demonstrate that you're coming from a place of concern and empathy.

There are also many smaller issues in the way people communicate that make it difficult to get the point across. Assumptions are frequent communication mistakes that can obscure the truth and discourage the other side from engaging further, especially when assumptions are seasoned with hostility, judgment, and other negative reactions. Assuming too much and jumping to conclusions is a force of habit for many people, and the antidote is listening while being patient.

Similarly, generalizations should also be avoided. The problem with generalizing things is that it obscures the finer details of the discussion. Generalizations can be avoided if you always remember to remember their positive traits and give your partner credit where it's due. For instance, if your partner has developed a bit of a gambling habit lately, you shouldn't let this one problem overshadow everything else you love about them. Acknowledging their positive traits will make them feel appreciated and more likely to listen to constructive criticism and advice.

Steps to Improve Communication

Putting aside mental health problems, it's always possible to learn how to communicate properly. This is true even for those who've had deep-seated issues throughout their lives and always struggled to communicate effectively. The overwhelming majority of people don't have what might be considered crippling communication issues, though. In most cases, it's a matter of some adjustment and exercise with the goal of improving their communicative skills. This is something that can be done without too much effort daily, and the following tips and exercises could be of help.

Creating Optimal Conditions

If you find it difficult to communicate with your significant other openly and without inhibitions, there are practical steps to set up optimal conditions for a conversation. When communication is particularly bad, talking about the problem is somewhat of a "Catch-22" situation since the problem itself requires a discussion. So serious discussions will go smoother if you and your partner put some effort into how, when, and where you'll talk.

For instance, timing is everything when you need to have a serious talk, and this is the case for couples at all levels of severity in their communication troubles. It goes without saying that some issues should not be raised in heated moments of tension. What's important is that both you and your partner discuss your issues with cool heads, so it's a good idea to ease into important conversations when you're having a particularly relaxed and comfortable time with each other.

The physical setting can play a huge role as well. Outside of therapy and counseling, this should be a private conversation at home or anywhere else you might find peace and quiet. Going to a calm and relaxing place with emotional significance for your relationship can also be beneficial. Lots of couples have places that they are attached to in some way, usually because it was the place where they met, spent some of their best times, or had some other pleasant memory associated with it.

The main goal should be to create a safe environment where both of you will be comfortable enough to open up and share your innermost feelings, thoughts, concerns, or anything else that can help sort things out. This applies to any topic or issue that needs to be resolved through conversation.

Communication in the Digital Era

It's no secret that the digital era and its many innovations have made it possible to communicate at dizzying speeds. This has had some dramatic effects on human relationships, romantic or otherwise, and that's not even the full impact yet.

Texting, for instance, is a very convenient way to keep in touch, but it can become overbearing in relationships. When you text too much all day, the habit can leave you worried when the slightest interruption in your texting streak occurs. However, research conducted at Pace University and presented by the American Psychological Association has shown that the way you text might be even more important than the frequency. Couples who text in a similar manner have reported greater relationship satisfaction.

Another issue with texting is that it sometimes affects avoidant behavior. For instance, avoiding a serious but uncomfortable discussion by bringing up one's phone is a common crutch. Instead of texting to avoid problems, you could perhaps use it as an opening for some of the conversations you need to have with your partner. If it's too difficult to say something, getting started over text and then picking it up from there could be very helpful. People used to do it with letters, so there is no reason it couldn't work via text.

Texting and social media may take away from the work that will help the relationship and communication flourish.

https://www.pexels.com/photo/round-table-and-white-table-cloth-3692887/

Social media and how couples behave on it have severe effects on relationships. Often, problems arise when someone takes issue with something their partner has posted. As a rule of thumb, ask yourself how you would feel if your partner posted something before making your own post. Furthermore, while you need personal boundaries, hiding your social media activity from your partner is never a good idea.

Communication Style Quiz

You've already learned some basic ways of assessing your and your partner's communication style, particularly via a checklist of habits, behaviors, and cues. However, individuals can have a million unique ways to communicate, so be as thorough as possible when identifying issues.

More detailed assessments can be very helpful in this regard, such as quizzes that will pose questions about how you communicate in specific situations. Below, you will find several useful questions that can help steer you toward learning more about how you and your partner communicate and where the issues might be, focusing on a few common situations that might occur in most relationships.

You've come home tired and have found that your partner hasn't finished a chore that was their responsibility. How do you react?

1. You reluctantly take care of the chore yourself and say nothing, dwelling on your annoyance.

2. You tell your partner that you've had a really long day and that you'd appreciate it if they would hold up their end of the deal when it comes to chores.

3. You start a fuss and attack your partner for not contributing enough while also throwing in a character attack, such as an accusation of laziness.

How do you deal with criticizing your partner about a mistake they've made?

1. The mistake annoys you, but you're afraid of being too critical and provoking an argument, so you let it slide.

2. You sit down for a comfortable evening with your significant other and casually ease into the conversation, voicing your concerns calmly and rationally.

3. You impulsively react to the mistake or bring it up randomly, perhaps as a weapon to use in an unrelated argument.

What's your usual reaction to financial disagreements, and how do you voice concerns about expenses?

1. You don't want to fight over money, so you say it's alright and move on, even though you're very worried about the impact on your budget.

2. You calmly raise your concern by asking your partner what they think and then state your case.

3. You call them irresponsible and immature.

What do you do when you have expectations and hopes for an upcoming anniversary or birthday?

1. You don't want to be a burden, so you say nothing and pray they'll meet your expectations.

2. You bring it up casually at a leisurely moment and drop a few clever hints.

3. You say nothing because you expect them to read your mind, but then you react with hostility if your expectations aren't met.

You want intimacy at a given moment, so you get your partner's attention in one of three ways.

1. You give them a few ambiguous hints or try to set the mood somehow, but you voice no intentions.

2. You gently move things in that direction and ask if your partner is in the mood.

3. You assume your partner is in the mood whenever you are, so you just grab them.

How do you communicate with your partner regarding your boundaries and alone time?

1. You are worried they might get jealous or feel unwanted, so you put up with too much control, eventually feeling trapped.

2. You explain to your partner that you sometimes need time for yourself and clarify what that entails.

3. You call them needy and shout at them to leave you alone.

One way to differentiate between various communication styles is to categorize them into three kinds. The first is the passive communication style, which is usually characterized by an aversion to conflict and reluctance to voice your opinions and concerns for fear of provoking a confrontation. This communication style leaves things unsaid and can lead to stonewalling, and it corresponds to the answers under number one in the above quiz. Answers under number two signify an assertive communication style. This is the optimal style because it allows for open communication and comfortable expression without aggression. Number three is the aggressive style, which carries all too familiar problems.

Role-reversal and Conflict Resolution Exercises

Last but not least, a simple yet effective empathy exercise is to reverse roles with your partner, at least in your head, when trying to understand their point of view. In relationships where one partner is the breadwinner, for instance, misunderstandings can often happen because the roles in the relationship are so different. If you or your partner can't understand why the other side feels a certain way, you should try your best to imagine yourself in their shoes.

There will be more details on cultivating empathy later in this book, but suffice it to say that role reversal can strengthen communication quite a bit. If the issue is with something simpler than earning a living, you can try to actually reverse roles for a while to see what insights you might get from the experience.

You can also do something similar in terms of conflict resolution. If you have a recurring conflict that keeps popping up, you can create an exercise around reenacting it. This is helpful because it can give you a level-headed perspective on what happens but without the actual drama. You can ask each other questions about what comes next after a typical action or statement and then try to understand why. It's likely that you'll see how silly some of the conflicts are because when you act it out, you will act as a kind of outside observer to your own problems.

Section 5: Resolving Past Issues

As previously hinted in this book, past issues in and outside your relationship can be a massive stumbling block in the way of communication, trust, empathy, and even love itself. These issues cover a wide spectrum of personal experiences that might transpire during your relationship, but they also include an infinite range of personal problems that you and your partner might have brought into the relationship.

Issues from the past that are unresolved can put a lot of negative pressure on your relationship.
https://www.pexels.com/photo/photo-of-a-woman-crouching-while-her-hands-are-on-her-head-5542968/

Past issues, no matter how bad they are, are no reason to despair, especially if they originate from experiences before you two met. When two people come together into a special romantic bond, they bring their entire beings and life stories into the mix. This is natural, and it's a good thing. The problems arise when unaddressed issues are allowed to fester somewhere under the surface until they grow to massive proportions. This section will teach you about past baggage and how to do your best to unburden yourself and your relationship.

The Impact of Past Problems and How to Isolate Them

To understand how the weight of the past can impact relationships, perhaps it is best to break these problems down into three main categories. Personal problems that have nothing to do with relationships, such as trauma, bad experiences from previous relationships, and long-term problems within the current relationship, can all manifest in a number of ways. Many methods for resolving these issues stand true across the categories, but problems need to be identified and understood before they are attempted to be solved.

These problems need to be acknowledged, identified, and addressed because they have a way of weighing down on a relationship and chipping away at it over time. They can lead to chronic tensions and impede your relationship's growth. This is mostly because obstacles will create insecurities and no-go areas regarding topics that can be discussed comfortably. Suppose a certain elephant in the room always produces instability whenever it's brought up. In that case, the foundations of the relationship can't be as stable as they need to be.

Generally, nothing should be left unresolved between two people who share their entire lives. Resolving such problems can be a delicate process, but with patience, communication, trust, and sometimes perhaps a bit of outside help, there's hardly anything you can't manage.

Personal Problems

When it comes to things like trauma, relationships aren't the only aspect of life that will be impacted. Whether it originates in childhood or later on in life, trauma will leave its imprint on the way a person thinks and articulates their emotions, as well as their overall behavior. It often produces problems with one's self-image, leading to negative outlooks on life, other people, and relationships. It's also important not to associate past trauma solely with extreme matters like childhood abuse. Trauma comes in all forms and can be traced to anything from experiences with abuse to bullying, social rejection, and others that can leave a lasting emotional scar on a person.

Signs that past trauma might be affecting your relationship include avoidance of certain topics and activities. This happens because things can come up that remind people of something bad that has happened, and there can be many triggers. That's why trauma makes it difficult to enjoy quality time with one's partner, sometimes in unexpected situations. Reacting with fear, anxiety, defensiveness, irritability, and various other negative emotions in situations where it doesn't make sense are all additional signs of trauma.

Past trauma also leads to disconnection, mistrust, and an overall problem with intimacy through no fault of the affected individual's romantic partner. Whatever difficult experiences you or your partner might have had, the residual effects can be overcome if you manage to get through to each other.

The Residue of Past Relationships

Long-term emotional baggage can also have to do with past relationships. There is a huge spectrum of things that can go wrong in a relationship, so people enter a new relationship with all sorts of negative past experiences. Abusive relationships, experiences with infidelity, a tough breakup, or a tragic loss of one's partner are some things that happen and leave a lasting scar on a person's love life.

While many issues can affect your relationship very similarly to past trauma, baggage from past relationships is much easier to talk about. Unless there was a particularly tragic episode or severe abuse involved, most people would be able to open up relatively easily in a safe space and talk about what they have experienced in a problematic past relationship. However, when they talk too much and too often about their ex, that's usually a sign that people are struggling to get over a past relationship. It doesn't necessarily mean they are still in love with their partner, miss them, or want to get back together. More often than not, it's simply emotional damage due to a failed relationship that hasn't been processed properly.

Hard breakups are probably the most common reason why people struggle to overcome their past relationships, as opposed to extreme cases such as abuse or tragedy. Emotional baggage can leave a person with self-esteem issues, feelings of personal failure, a loss of hope, and a reluctance to truly open up to the prospect of happiness in a new relationship.

Past Burdens Within Your Relationship

Long-standing issues that drag on for years in a relationship result from unaddressed problems that are ignored for one reason or another. This goes back to what you've learned about communication, trust, and intimacy. Whenever you and your partner have a concern that you choose to sweep under the rug to avoid a discussion or because you're feeling insecure, you risk laying the foundations for chronic conflict. This is a very unfortunate state of affairs because, more often than not, these things can be resolved through conversation.

Of course, past transgressions are also the source of long-term resentment and tensions. If the relationship survives, couples will sometimes appear to move on from past dishonesty, infidelity, and similar slights, but the healing process isn't always complete. These issues require thorough processing and must be dealt with openly and thoroughly to be truly resolved. For instance, superficially forgiving mistakes without rebuilding trust is a flimsy foundation on which to build the relationship's future.

Letting Go of the Weight

Everything you've learned in the previous chapters can play a role in resolving past issues with your partner. To open up about these problems (especially deeply rooted personal issues like trauma) requires trust. Even arriving at the topic requires intimacy. Knowing how to resolve conflicts will help minimize the destructive effects of past problems while you work to resolve them. The most important prerequisite, of course, is communication, without which none of these things are possible.

Signs of Trouble

It's always a good first step to ensure that past problems are the real issue troubling your relationship. People can have problems and still function relatively well in relationships, with other areas of the relationship being higher priorities to fix. There are signs to look out for when determining if the main problem lies in your relationship's past.

A common symptom is when a certain problem or topic repeatedly arises during an argument. It can also linger around in normal interactions without necessarily provoking a major argument. Snarky remarks, constantly bringing up the past, taking jabs at each other, and being judgmental about a specific thing from the past are signs of unresolved issues between you and your partner. People who've gotten over past problems might sometimes joke about the past, and this is healthy if it's sincerely just poking fun. However, if there are any hostile undertones, an individual is likely bothered by something.

It will be relatively easy to notice if a past relationship interferes with your current one. Mistrust and communication problems are common symptoms, but the treatment of the current relationship can also be quite telling. Sometimes, people will enter a relationship as an attempt to get over a previous one, and this often happens on a subconscious level. They'll often assume things about you incorrectly and find it difficult to accept that relationships will naturally run into problems. They will create patterns that remind them of their previous relationship, and any current hiccups will lead to frustration instead of a genuine desire to fix it. This is because, for these individuals, the new relationship is a coping mechanism, and they expect it to fix all of their problems.

Getting over Past Transgressions

What you should understand first and foremost is that all relationships will eventually run into some kind of problem and that all of your feelings have validity. Just like topics of discussion, emotions should not be made taboo. If your partner has done something to hurt you or betray your trust in the past, it's natural to feel disappointment or anger with them. It's normal to even reconsider the entire relationship. Still, once you allow yourself to feel your own emotions with sincerity, you'll open the door to the realization that this doesn't have to be the end.

The longer you bury the past, the more internal unresolved issues you will have that will reflect on your relationship.

It's impossible to reconcile with things that you intentionally bury. Think about when you might have been in a fight with a friend, coworker, or someone else to a point where you are no longer on speaking terms. If you've had these experiences and managed to resolve the problem, then you know reconciliation only came after you started talking again. On the other hand, living with someone you care about and continuing to communicate without addressing a serious issue is even less productive than breaking off contact.

When people get angry with each other and cease interacting, they at least know where they stand. The problem is obvious, and the breakdown is over, so it's easier to know what should be done if the relationship is to be healed. Pretending that everything is fine eliminates clarity, muddies the waters, and makes the situation much more difficult to handle.

Anger and disappointment can be addressed and prevented from becoming unbearable resentment over time. When you clearly communicate your feelings to your partner, they are more likely to understand the full impact of their actions, which will motivate them to correct their wrongs or at least ask you what they can do to correct them. Like relationships, people are likely to be imperfect and naturally make mistakes. The trick is to accept and work with them because, at the end of the day, there are all those reasons why you care about them and your relationship.

Forgiveness

That's where forgiveness comes into play. Some people find forgiveness more difficult than others, but everyone can do it for the right person. The important thing is for forgiveness to be genuine, but often, it's possible to think that you've forgiven your partner without truly getting over it, resulting in prolonged bitterness and instability. The way to avoid this is by being honest about your feelings, with yourself first and foremost. This is why valuing your emotions and being open about them is necessary.

Instead of just saying it's fine and rushing to move on to another topic, you should always try to elaborate on your forgiveness and what it really entails. Articulate exactly what troubles you, why you're forgiving your partner, and how you would like to proceed. These words can be more impactful when externalized by being written down, so it's a good idea to write something like a forgiveness letter, which you can try in the space below. If you just need to articulate your feelings, you might choose to keep the letter to yourself, but if you decide to give it to your partner, it can be a great conversation starter.

_____
_____
_____
_____
_____
_____
_____
_____
_____
_____
_____
_____
_____
_____

Reversing Roles via the Empty Chair Technique

As always, reversing roles with your partner and role-playing to study past conflicts can be a great exercise to strengthen your empathy for each other. You might want to explore some aspects of Gestalt therapy, such as the so-called empty chair technique. Gestalt therapy is a holistic approach that focuses on helping individuals gain better insight into themselves, emphasizing their environment, experiences, and relationships. The idea is for patients to understand why they're doing certain things and what they can do to change while also finding inner peace through self-acceptance.

The empty chair technique is all about tackling unresolved feelings and conflicts. The exercise is carried out by instructing an individual to have an imaginary talk with someone by imagining that they are sitting in the empty chair in front of them. Similarly to writing a forgiveness letter, this technique externalizes your inner conflicts and unaddressed feelings you need to articulate. In some sessions, patients might also be instructed to have a conversation with a part of their own personality.

The Empty Chair Technique is a monologue imagined as a dialogue.
https://www.pexels.com/photo/filled-white-coffee-cup-on-saucer-261698/

This is essentially a monologue imagined as a dialogue, and the goal is to talk as clearly and openly as possible to the "person" you're in conflict with. The technique is especially helpful as a precursor if you're still struggling to have a real open conversation with your partner. Simply sit in front of an empty chair, imagine your partner or a part of yourself struggling with past grief, and try to explain your emotions, thoughts, and the way you see your current predicament in as much detail as possible.

After you've stated your case, you can sit in the empty chair, doing your best to respond to what you have just said. These exercises are usually done in the presence of a therapist, but they can also be very helpful on your own. It's a good idea to get a notebook, write down a few bullet points of what you've said before switching chairs, and then address the list from the other side. If you do this enough times, you might be surprised by how much you'll learn about both perspectives just by externalizing your problems verbally.

Stronger Together

Whatever past weight you and your significant other might carry, working together is the only way to unburden your relationship. Depending on your problem, it might require a lot of patience, understanding, and diligent emotional work. As intimate and committed as people in love might be, it's also true that not everyone is equipped with the skills needed to address some of those particularly big personal problems. Sometimes, a bit of outside assistance is just what a couple needs to start moving in the right direction. However, so much can still be done if you and your partner understand each other's needs.

Dealing with Personal Problems

If you and your partner are going to work on a deep, personal problem from the past by yourselves, the healing might take a lot of effort and become an arduous process. When someone struggles with past trauma, it's rarely going to be enough to just sit down for one conversation. You need to create a safe space within your relationship where there will be no judgment and negativity.

You can do this by establishing a set of shared activities you both enjoy, focusing on making them therapeutic and as comfortable as possible. The greatest work, however, will be in applying everything you've learned in the previous sections about building trust and intimacy and improving your communication. Improving any of these aspects of your relationship will make the struggling spouse/partner more comfortable and secure.

It's not always a good idea to jump right into the most difficult conversations and open up all the wounds at once. Facing problems head-on and tackling the full extent of the pain immediately works for some people. Still, it can be incredibly difficult or even counterproductive for others. You should consider an approach similar to what you'll find in exposure therapy, which is often used to treat phobias. Exposing yourself or your partner to painful conversations in small bits, incrementally increasing in severity, can help retain a semblance of comfort while opening up. The idea is to gradually build up tolerance and garner strength to explore further.

Gratitude and Trust

Gratitude is an invaluable aspect of healing from any setbacks in life, and it includes the gratitude you and your partner feel toward each other, as well as being thankful for everything good in your lives overall. You should incorporate gratitude into how you communicate with your partner regularly, always trying to focus on the positives. This will help both of you feel more appreciated and validated while also reminding you how far you've come and why your relationship is so valuable despite what might have happened in the past. Contrast is powerful, and focusing on what's good can help put problems into perspective, making them seem less intimidating.

The importance of trust can also never be overstated. Without trust, it can be impossible to truly move on from past mistakes. It's impossible to open up, making it difficult to address personal problems or talk about the issues. The more you work on trust, the more doors will open between you and your partner, and you'll find that more and more pieces will spontaneously start coming together.

Seeking Professional Help

Dealing with the past and truly moving on from it can be seen as an endeavor combining the things you've learned about in this book thus far. Building trust, nurturing intimacy, communicating openly, and constructively navigating your conflicts will help you tackle any problems that life throws at your relationship, let alone problems that have occurred in the past.

However, a troubled past can also damage a person's mental health. If necessary, you and your significant other should sit down and discuss whether it's time to seek outside counsel. Therapy is a great step toward recovery, and preparing for it by covering the topic extensively with your partner will help you get the most out of it if you decide to go in that direction.

Section 6: Individuality – Why It Matters

The difference between individuality and collectivism is one of the oldest dichotomies of the human experience, or at least it's presented as such. These two aspects of human social behavior don't necessarily have to be at odds. Even though it might seem counterintuitive at first, since relationships entail two people coming together and connecting, individuality actually plays a prominent role in relationships. This section will explore the concept of individuality in more detail, particularly concerning its place within romantic relationships and how to make the most of it to achieve balance between yourself and your partner.

Individuality is something that will add to the value and strength of your relationship.
https://www.pexels.com/photo/young-woman-painting-on-paper-at-workplace-3771055/

False Dichotomies and the Importance of Individuality in Relationships

If you've ever felt like individuality and togetherness are at odds with each other, try to consider what brought you and your partner together in the first place. However it happened, you certainly didn't bump into each other in the street and agree to relinquish your identities and morph into a collective mind! On the contrary, you clicked because you saw certain things you liked about each other.

You can define individuality in a few ways – *but understand that it has nothing to do with selfishness or egocentricity.* The simplest and most common definition says that individuality relates to the qualities and character of a person, particularly in the sense that these things distinguish them from other people. So, individuality is simply about the things that make you unique as a person, no matter how small and seemingly insignificant those things are. It just means you're different, not necessarily separate, and certainly not isolated.

A healthy sense of individuality enables a person to maintain an awareness of their unique qualities and traits without making them feel alienated, interfering with their ability to connect, or causing them to shun the idea of belonging to a team or a community. Your individuality includes all those things you bring to the table when you enter a relationship, and those things are usually what attracts someone to you in the first place.

Individuality is one of the main ingredients in making relationships fulfilling, dynamic, and satisfying. People who hold onto their individuality will maintain their personal identity and all the good things it includes. As such, relationships where individuality is preserved and cherished will enable the couple to enjoy much more of each other. Relationships require more than just two people who make every effort to be copies of each other in order to be dynamic and fulfilling. One of the reasons two people in love can interact so vibrantly is that they have all those small differences, quirks, and thoughts that they find attractive about each other. Of course, many relationships are built on shared interests, and a sense of connection comes from things two people have in common, but the new things they discover about each other along the way are the finest spice.

It's such a major and possibly destructive misconception that partners must share every interest and perspective. While there is some truth in that, many people have found the opposite to be true, which is why popular wisdom also suggests that opposites attract. Your partner is someone you can learn from and who can help you grow as a person, which are some of the most valuable benefits of getting involved in an intimate relationship in the first place.

The key takeaway here is that individuality defines your character's uniqueness and your willingness to maintain that identity. It means being different and being who you are, not being separate or selfish. Even the most consolidated collectives can be made up of people who are strong individuals, and relationships are no exception. Despite common misconceptions, being in a relationship does not require sacrificing your identity and molding yourself into a perfect image that you think is expected of you, nor will this even benefit the relationship.

Relationships entail compromises, of course, but those compromises work best when they are agreed upon by two people who respect each other and are open about what they feel and think. There is thus no mutual exclusivity or contradiction between individuality and collectivism, especially not in relationships. However, striking a fine balance between the two is the key to a healthy relationship. On the extreme ends of this spectrum, individuality can certainly lead to selfishness or egocentrism, while eliminating individuality can lead to dissatisfaction, emotional suffocation, and feelings of being controlled and stripped of your identity.

For a relationship to remain stable, it's crucial that both partners feel affirmed and validated. This means feeling that you are being supported in your efforts and encouraged to be the person you are instead of being judged, controlled, and reshaped in someone else's image. Individuality in relationships has much to do with mutual respect, which comes naturally for most people when they love someone. Unfortunately, personal insecurities sometimes cause people to be more controlling and distrustful of their partner.

None of this is to say that people who are in relationships should always remain completely unchanged over the years. Individuality is more than holding on to every single trait you have and never making a compromise. There is a big difference between controlling someone and encouraging them to improve and achieve their full potential. Healthy relationships tend to gradually move people toward changing for the better, which primarily entails self-improvement.

A supportive partner who truly understands you will awaken your desire to improve yourself and your life, which means building something good on a foundation already there. That foundation is the essence of your identity and what constitutes your individuality. Your essence is what your partner falls in love with, so their respect for who you are comes spontaneously. Their attempts to motivate you to better yourself aren't an infringement on your individuality or an attempt to control you but rather an attempt to keep your spark untarnished.

This positive influence amounts to supportiveness, but the line can sometimes get blurry. This usually happens when there is a communication breakdown, and you fail to clarify boundaries and express your needs. That's how communication plays an integral part in balancing individuality and togetherness. Your partner must understand which parts of your identity you want to cherish and which problems are keeping you down. Only then can they help you become a better version of yourself instead of abandoning your identity.

Balance and the Benefits Gained from Individuality in Relationships

The benefits of individuality in your relationship are more important than you might think. A relationship between two people who respect each other's individuality will certainly be more stimulating, but it's about much more than just excitement and fun.

The fact that partners in a romantic relationship can help each other grow and reach their potential, for instance, is why individuality should not be dismissed. Hobbies are a very good example of this because of their potential. Suppose you require your partner to forego the hobbies they are passionate about. In that case, they won't just become more dissatisfied with their lives. Hobbies that people are passionate about are fulfilling, but they also have the potential to grow and develop into incredible careers, and they offer many other opportunities. If you demand that your partner relinquish this aspect of their individuality, you will directly stifle their potential for personal growth.

Working on your individual strengths can actually bring you closer together.
https://www.pexels.com/photo/photo-of-two-people-using-their-gadgets-4065137/

As people grow toward their true potential, they also bring more to the relationship. Their passion and happiness will reflect on their partner, and they will become more confident, content, and self-aware. All those things learned along the way make each person's journey so inspiring! The new knowledge, skills, and perspectives they'll pick up along that road will be invaluable to their relationships.

People who maintain their identity and are allowed to blossom to the best of their abilities will naturally be better at communicating. They will know themselves and possess a certain inner peace that stems from confidence and fulfillment. This is the stuff that healthy relationships are made of, and individuality plays a decisive role in making that possible.

Individuality is also one of the ingredients in independence and self-reliance. Being overly dependent on each other is a common pitfall for couples in romantic relationships, and it happens as a result of too much control and too many compromises on what makes you who you are. A loving relationship is all about support and sharing, not control and domination.

The Balancing Act

Having a healthy relationship is, in many ways, a balancing act. One of the clearest examples is positioning yourself in that golden middle between maintaining your individuality and making contributions and sacrifices to your relationship. If you truly internalize the idea that you should encourage your partner's personal growth and get the same support in return, you will quickly understand a vital aspect of achieving that balance.

In practical terms, it's setting basic personal boundaries, respecting each other's need for personal space and autonomy, and encouraging the pursuit of each other's hobbies and long-term goals in life. A simple mental exercise for people who share their lives with a significant other is to see it as having two identities. One identity is who you are as a person, which includes your character but also your passions and goals, while the other identity is the couple.

This simple dichotomy will help you understand what you need to do to maintain your identity while doing what is necessary to make your relationship work. To understand where your identity begins and the couple's ends and what your personal boundaries should be, ask yourself simple questions about who you are. Central questions are what you find important, which thoughts and feelings you are unwilling to relinquish, what your values are, which friendships you hold dear, what you need in life, and which interests or hobbies you don't want to give up.

Not being able to answer these questions leads people to relinquish their individuality and become overly dependent on their partner. Once you know who you are and where you are going, you will have a clear outline of what makes you who you are, and you will find that a loving, supportive partner will respect that. The ultimate goal is to balance these things with the knowledge you've learned in the previous sections, such as trust, openness, intimacy, and the common long-term goals of your relationship.

Cherishing Individuality in Your Relationship

Now that you understand how individuality plays into romantic relationships, you can see its potential to make your shared life more fulfilling. There are numerous ways individuality might fit into your particular relationship since every couple is unique in some ways. How you and your partner or spouse incorporate individuality into your lives depends on your characters, needs, expectations, and countless other personal factors that only you will know. Some couples will naturally express less individuality because they might not need it as much. Still, everyone can try a few things to see the positive effects individuality can have on their relationships. The following tips and exercises will help you strengthen the role of individuality between you and your partner.

Setting Goals

Since personal goals are a crucial aspect of your individuality and that of your partner, this is an area where you can practice respecting each other's individuality and becoming more comfortable with it. Partners in a healthy relationship should already have a clear idea of their needs and goals. That's why it's relatively easy for them to set personal goals that don't interfere with the needs of their partnership. A couple should use communication to establish their expectations and what their relationship needs to function and flourish. They can encourage each other to set personal goals when proper communication and trust are established.

You and your partner should have open discussions about what personal goals you might want to set for each other. At the same time, you should also discuss how you can support each other in achieving those goals. With a strong support system, personal goals might even take on the form of a joint endeavor. Encouraging and helping each other to achieve those goals is one of the highest statements of balance between individuality and togetherness.

This is why support for personal undertakings and ambition feels so validating. It strengthens the feeling of appreciation and respect while also reinforcing trust. Relationships are also about guidance, so this doesn't mean giving unconditional support without input to every idea one of you has. Through honest discussions, however, it's always possible to smooth things out and figure out the best course.

You can always support the goal while having a few things to say about the proposed road toward that goal. For example, suppose your partner wants to change career paths or become an entrepreneur. In that case, this goal is definitely worthy of support. However, if they want to quit their job immediately without setting a new path for themselves, it may or may not be a good idea. It is important to discuss it and ensure your partner's personal goals are taken seriously and encouraged.

Allocating Personal Space

Most people will need at least a bit of personal space at some point, and this is another common expression of individuality. There are activities that some people enjoy and get the most out of only when they're on their own, which is natural. There are also those thoughts and feelings that are sometimes best resolved through some good old-fashioned soul-searching. At first glance, it might seem difficult to differentiate between a plain need for personal space and a communication problem. If your partner wants to do something independently, you might misconstrue that as stonewalling or avoidance. However, these misunderstandings will only happen if there are insecurities and poor communication in your relationship *to begin with.*

If you are patient and open-minded, it will be easy to discuss these things with your partner and realize that their need for some personal space doesn't mean something is wrong between you. It's also beneficial to create a personal space plan together by agreeing on separate times for being alone; this will help avoid co-dependency. This course is good if you're simultaneously resolving your communication issues and building trust. If you sit down and make a schedule that allocates and clearly defines personal space, there will be no surprises and uncomfortable moments that need explaining. Spontaneity has its own charms, of course, but for struggling couples, it's best to keep it within the confines of shared activities and quality time you spend together.

Exploring Interests

You can also encourage each other to explore new interests and activities to introduce more individuality into the relationship. Sometimes, you or your partner might feel like you've been neglecting your individuality simply due to a lack of effort, not necessarily because you have been trying to control the other. This can lead to just as much dissatisfaction with life, which also reflects on the relationship.

Sometimes, it's necessary to give your partner a push to encourage and cherish each other's individuality. This joint exercise could bring quite a bit of novelty and excitement into your lives. For instance, you can sit down and talk to each other about what kinds of new hobbies, interests, and activities you might be interested in but have never tried. You should engage in these activities independently and in your own personal time. After you try these new hobbies, you can share your experiences with each other.

These novelties can produce interesting conversations, and you might also learn new things about each other. It could be that you or your partner used to consider individuality as something unwanted or detrimental to your relationship, so you never brought up certain interests you would have liked to explore. Once you understand that personal pursuits can fit into a relationship, you might find yourselves unlocking new and exciting areas in your lives.

Getting excited about new things, enjoying some freedom, and then returning home to share your excitement and passion could be a very rejuvenating experience for your relationship. When creating a list or discussing these new personal activities, go into some detail on what the activities might entail. More precisely, it's always good to let your partner know what they're in for, particularly if a new hobby requires considerable financial or otherwise investment.

Establishing Boundaries

Finally, it's worth reiterating the importance of personal boundaries in a functional relationship. Communicating about the issue is the simplest and perhaps most important exercise. Unfortunately, the topic of personal boundaries arises only after one of the partners in the relationship starts to feel that theirs has been violated. If you and your partner can talk openly about how you feel, this isn't a major issue because you know you can just sit down and smooth things out.

However, it's best to prevent these feelings from happening in the first place by setting personal boundaries within the relationship ahead of time. When discussing this with your partner, your goal should be to clearly define areas of your life where you truly feel you need to handle things independently. You must differentiate between personal boundaries and the urge to avoid certain topics or activities with your partner. If you have a problem, especially concerning the relationship, your "personal boundary" should never be to keep it to yourself.

Personal boundaries usually concern things that aren't very consequential for your relationship, such as having a private office at home or spending time with a friend. Whatever your boundaries, you should talk about them openly with your partner and identify them as clearly as possible. Your partner should also be given the opportunity to do the same. If you struggle with giving each other personal space and find each other overbearing, you can start with minor steps.

For instance, going to the mall and then separating to run your own errands or do your shopping can be a valuable yet easy exercise. These activities reinforce the idea that you can handle things separately and make your own decisions before returning *home together.*

Section 7: Planning Your Future

The matter of individuality in relationships and the balance between it and togetherness also feeds into what this section will focus on. Every relationship should focus on the future for two main reasons. Firstly, long-term relationships are always built with at least some foresight and consideration for where things might go. People who don't make future considerations when getting romantically involved don't end up in serious and ongoing relationships, either by choice or as a spontaneous consequence of how they live. Secondly, the future, in general, is a major factor in how a relationship develops.

Planning a healthy future together takes communication and compromise.

So, planning for the future is something that every couple should know how to do. How you make plans and adapt to unforeseen developments can make or break what you've been building in your relationship. This section will explore how your future plays a part in your relationship, how to make plans to ensure that things go smoothly in the future, and a few tips on how to get better at planning in general.

Alignment with Your Partner

Couples tend to have multiple visions for the future, focusing on different aspects of life. For one, everyone has at least a basic vision for their own personal future, no matter how basic of an outline it might be. Everybody has at least a few things they'd like or wouldn't like to see in their lives years later. Then, there are the future expectations that relate specifically to the relationship, which can also be seen as the relationship's needs.

In relationships, aligning your long-term goals with your partner's is paramount. Finding common ground between your shared vision for your relationship's future and your individual dreams and goals is another crucial balancing act you must focus on. Suppose your individual goals don't fit in with what your relationship will require. In that case, it's difficult to maintain stability in the long term. Being too self-centered and putting your needs before the relationship is one of the surest ways of eroding and eventually destroying a relationship. On the other hand, sacrificing too many personal goals can lead to chronic discontent, friction, and even resentment. Both of these extremes are equally detrimental.

Aligning your personal goals and dreams with your partner and relationship is an exercise that can be different from one couple to another. Still, there are a few general rules that you should follow. These mostly involve self-reflection because alignment starts with you and your partner individually. You can't make decisions for each other or tell each other what goals you should pursue, so both of you need to start in your own backyard, so to speak.

The first step in that direction is to take a good look inside yourself and make sure that you know where you're headed in the first place. Being goal-oriented and following a clear path is one of the best recipes for long-term stability overall, which translates into relationships. Nobody can control everything that life throws their way, but main goals can be set well in advance. If you and your partner know each other's passions and dreams, it will be easier to make decisions together while ensuring they are in line with the relationship's goals.

Similarly, it's beneficial to understand your values and core beliefs, especially regarding relationships, while communicating them clearly to your partner. Couples who are clear on their individual values will have an easier time aligning with each other in the long term because it'll be easier to articulate their expectations. For instance, if you're trying to envision a future for your relationship, consider where you stand on things like marriage or having kids.

Some people will maintain a serious, long-term relationship even if they don't want marriage, but that's still a decision they've arrived at by thinking about the future and articulating their personal views on relationships. Knowing exactly what you want and don't want for your relationship will make it possible to keep your partner informed on where you stand. Problems usually emerge when this topic isn't given its due thought and consideration, leaving things ambiguous and strained. Without information, your partner will be left guessing and probably start to unconsciously fill in the blanks. This can build up assumptions or expectations that might catch you off guard when you least expect them, and the sudden realization of mismatched and unsaid expectations is a rather common cause of breakups.

At the end of the day, aligning your individual dreams and goals in the relationship boils down to articulating said goals, transparency, communication, and a bit of compromise. Remember that this alignment is an ongoing process that you'll need to maintain over time. Decisions and new directions, which are certain to come, need to be reviewed and adjusted if needed.

While you and your partner should respect each other's personal goals, every decision for the future should be evaluated within the context of the relationship. When contemplating a plan or any other long-term decision, always ask yourself how it will affect the relationship, how it fits into your shared vision as a couple, and whether it's compatible. There is no reason to reflect on these things silently. The more you consult with your partner and share feedback, the lower the chances of future complications.

During that process, you may run into certain differences. Regardless of how well you get along, you and your significant other will sometimes see certain things differently. However, these differences won't be a major obstacle if they don't relate to the nature of your relationship on a fundamental level. You can disagree on finances, career paths, or where to live, but surface issues are easy to resolve if you're on the same frequency regarding where your relationship is headed and what it means to you.

If you maintain open lines of communication, intimacy, and trust, there are very few disagreements you won't be able to negotiate through as long as you both have the same expectations or at least a clear compromise on how you see your relationship developing over the years.

Working Together

Planning for the future is integral to every healthy and fulfilling relationship. The benefit isn't only in having a clear plan and a secure long-term path, though. Working on these plans together brings couples closer and is one of the best ways to improve the relationship overall. Planning for your future as a couple also has the added effect of putting your relationship in perspective and reminding you of what you're working toward.

Setting goals, in general, is a good way to strengthen a sense of purpose in what you're doing. This is easily felt individually, even when you set small goals only a few days ahead. Having a clear long-term goal in life, however, is a well-known and useful tool for keeping yourself focused and motivated. In that regard, relationships are a lot like individuals. The purpose is indeed easier to find when you're with someone you love, but making plans and talking about all those good things that the two of you want in the future will only strengthen your resolve.

Getting on the Same Page

Joining forces and consulting each other when making future plans will reinforce trust and elevate the confidence that both of you have in the relationship. This is because the very act of talking about your shared future demonstrates to both of you that the other side factors in the relationship when making any decisions for the future. It acknowledges your commitment to the relationship and makes it clear that your relationship is something you both hold dear and have no intention of abandoning.

It takes constant discussions and planning to really see where you want to go together in your future plans.

If you've never spent much time discussing the future with your partner, breaking the ice might initially be a little jarring. A common inhibition people have is worrying that they'll come across as needy and incessant toward their partner, possibly pressuring them too much and ultimately driving them away. In healthy relationships, mentioning the future and expressing your expectations is never a problem. This is especially true if the inquiring partner makes sure they ask the other side for their thoughts and feedback, giving room for constructive back-and-forth.

However, if communicating on this level is an issue in your relationship, gradually ease into the topic. You don't necessarily have to jump straight into the traditional "Where do you see us in five years?" type of questions. A good entry point is casually bringing up things like hopes, dreams, ambitions, career goals, and other future paths that your partner might have without referring to your relationship specifically.

When you get your partner talking, encourage them to discuss what they want to do with their life. It won't take long before you can gauge certain hints about how much your relationship factors in for your partner's future planning. Suppose you're already on the same page in terms of emotional investment. In that case, they'll probably bring it up on their own by pointing out how your relationship fits into their plans. Honesty plays a crucial role in these discussions, as there is no other way for the two of you to ascertain where you stand.

Once the discussion undoubtedly moves on to your relationship's future, you can outline your individual visions. This means doing your best to harmonize your potentially different points of view. The starting point is an agreement that you both care and want to build your relationship in the future, after which you'll determine if adjustments need to be made to your plans.

Individuality and the Power of Support

Your best strategy for harmonizing your visions for the future is extensive communication. You must listen closely to your partner and be honest and open. One of the best ways to foster understanding is to help each other articulate your goals, including career paths, family life, overall lifestyle, and personal growth.

If one of you struggles to articulate personal goals (and no verbal encouragement seems to help), your best bet is to externalize the mental process via paper.

As in previously mentioned exercises, things like lists and simple quizzes can do wonders to make sense of jumbled thoughts. You can start with something very simplistic, such as basic lists of desires in different categories like work, education, lifestyle, and anything relevant.

Once you have listed those desires, you and your partner can determine the practical steps toward fulfillment. When you start getting ideas, you'll find it easy to analyze how those plans will fit your relationship goals. This is the simplest path toward getting you and your partner on the same frequency and helping you decide which compromises to make and when.

As previously discussed, relationships will benefit from preserving the partners' individuality, including future planning. Romantic relationships are a force of nature, but they also make some of the best support systems you can find. Similarly, to the family you come from, especially parents, the support you do or don't get from your partner can affect you as an individual.

Striking the perfect balance between compromises and individual aspirations will enable you to give each other the best support while keeping your relationship stable. As the two of you explore the future and your plans in more and more detail over time, you may find all sorts of unexpected inspirations, interests, and passions. Romantic partners have a way of awakening these things in each other and realizing that someone intimately close to you is there to support you and can be a strong wind on your back.

Practical Planning and Setting Goals

To set up practical long-term goals together as a team, you and your partner will need to communicate about the future consistently and openly. Relationships, where everything is out in the open without inhibition, will have the easiest time adjusting to changes and standing the test of time. This is especially true regarding goals and plans because it ensures no major surprises lead to instability.

Ideally, you and your partner should never end up in a situation where one surprises the other with a major and sudden shift in their life goals, especially a shift that can impact the relationship. When you talk openly about your passions, expectations, dreams, and ideas, it's very unlikely that this will ever happen. Important decisions that can affect the relationship should always be made together, taking input from both sides. Knowing how to plan more effectively and cover all your bases in different areas of life is necessary.

The point to take home is that you and your partner should work in unison whenever possible. Leave room for individuality where you can, but take advantage of the fact that two minds are stronger than one whenever you're considering the growth of your relationship. Your first step should be to identify your priorities as a couple by making a list of goals that you agree on. These goals include everything from buying a car to getting married and having children.

As you would when trying to help each other articulate your personal goals, making common, united goals as a couple can also benefit from the written form. Setting aside a few hours every week to explore this topic in detail during a quiet evening at home with your partner can be helpful. Goals should be as straightforward and comprehensive as possible to make it easier to stay focused.

For instance, they can consist of three properties, including the goal's category, a brief description of the goal itself, and one or more actions to be taken toward that goal. Common categories are finances, professional life, lifestyle, family, health, or personal growth. To articulate these goals with your partner, use a simple goal-setting template. Perhaps you and your partner have decided to improve your health or fitness. You might open the template with a fitness category and create a corresponding goal, such as running one mile daily. That simple goal can require various actions, such as buying running shoes or finding a suitable area. The same principle applies to more complex, long-term goals. Something else to consider is that united goals can still leave room for individual action. Suppose you and your partner have the common goal of buying a house. Joining forces to achieve that goal means task allocation between you, such as you looking for options and your partner contacting the respective real estate agencies. While buying the house is a common goal, the finer details of the plan are made up of what you might consider to be personal goals for both of you.

While fitness is a convenient example, the above methods can apply to any long-term goals in your relationship. The more you practice planning and goal-setting with your partner on regular, everyday activities, the more natural it'll become for you to make plans together. Communication and intimacy will benefit immensely from these activities, and you might not even realize that you're gradually becoming much more comfortable with each other and the future. It's also guaranteed that any changes and plans you make will be much easier to accomplish with your significant other at your side.

Whatever your goals, to get your priorities right and motivate yourself to stick to the plan, using a vision board might also be a good idea. A vision or dream board is a simple and creative endeavor that usually entails a collage of pictures, other visuals, affirmative messages, and important goals or reminders. It can be a fun, leisurely activity when you and your partner spend your free time together. Your vision board will be unique to your life, but its objective is to inspire and motivate both of you.

You can create a vision board that more broadly refers to your relationship and its goals, or it can consist of something more specific, such as your united journey toward physical fitness or anything else you're working on together. Making a vision board is easy and requires little time or materials. A sizeable bulletin board works perfectly because it provides plenty of space to thoroughly personalize the board with photos, catchphrases, reminders, written priorities, and much else.

Creating a vision board doesn't have to be a one-time exercise. If your board has enough space, things can be added later on. Putting it up at a prominent place in your home creates a shared place of casual expression for you and your partner. It's a collage of ideas where you can put up new plans and a pin in things you'd like to see in the future.

Your vision board can be a way to create pleasant surprises for your partner. For instance, a sudden idea you've had for a vacation spot can go up on the vision board and brighten up your partner's day when they see it. If you have your board up for a long time, it can also become a humble collage of memories and feelings. Thoughts, feelings, and affirmative messages you pin for each other can catch your attention again a couple of years later and be a pleasant reminder of the things that matter.

The most valuable message to internalize is that your plans are only as good as your communication with each other. The more you discuss your plans and explore their finer details with a strong regard for each other's input, the more feasible and consistent your plans will be. There will be less room for mistakes and unpleasant surprises if you and your partner clearly know what the other expects from your plans and why. As long as you are in complete harmony and clarity as to the ultimate goals of your relationship, you will both have an easy time making all the necessary compromises.

Section 8: Cultivating Empathy

In the long term, empathy will be one of the most powerful factors in maintaining and keeping your relationship stable. Empathy is an inherent human trait that has played a crucial role in helping people survive and thrive. More precisely, the ability to organize and communicate on such a uniquely sophisticated level has been the deciding factor in most of the major human accomplishments throughout history. *And a lot of that is thanks to people's ability to empathize with each other.*

Empathy is an ongoing task you must work on with your partner throughout your life.

Empathy's importance cannot be overstated; it makes it possible to understand your partner, communicate effectively, resolve conflicts, and make plans together. When couples can effectively empathize with each other, they can resolve most problems easily. Still, sometimes, *empathy itself is the problematic area that needs attention.* This section will take a deep dive into the concept of empathy, why it matters so much, and what you can do to improve it.

The Definition and Nature of Empathy

In the simplest terms, empathy is all about emotional understanding between people. It allows you to recognize certain emotions in others, whether basic and visible things like fear or something more subtle and complex, like envy. The greater the range of emotions one can recognize in others, the more empathetic they are. Empathy makes it possible to put yourself in someone else's figurative shoes and imagine, as accurately as possible, what they might be going through.

Empathy is an unspoken yet universal human language deeply rooted in evolution. The ideas around empathy have certainly absorbed some societal and cultural influence across different times and spaces, but the underlying ability is biological and has been around for a very long time. The presence of cruelty and all manner of malice in the world certainly poses the question of why empathy sometimes appears to be absent in people, given that it comes so naturally to the majority. Given all these factors, empathy has been studied quite a bit over the years.

Scientific research into empathy goes back more than a hundred years (to 1909) and the work of psychologist Edward B. Titchener. Since then, different scientific disciplines have proposed theories and explanations as to where empathy comes from. In neuroscience, more recent research has shown that certain parts of the human brain are particularly active in relation to empathy, such as the anterior insula and the anterior cingulate cortex.

This research doesn't necessarily explain why humans have empathy, but it makes it quite clear that it's at least partly a neurobiological process. Scans have also shown the involvement of the inferior frontal gyrus in the process of empathy. Further reinforcing the theory of empathy as a natural occurrence is that damage to the IFG can hinder a person's ability to recognize the emotions behind other people's facial expressions and, in turn, connect with them.

Other explanations and theories about empathy are mostly emotional and social. Adam Smith, for instance, theorized that the purpose of empathy was partly to improve people's emotional depth through the experience of feeling the emotions of others. Having such a wide range of emotional experiences, via your own experiences and those of others, would thus serve to train you emotionally. Since people can empathize with real and fictional characters, they can experience many emotions they may not encounter alone.

Viewing empathy through a sociological lens offers a more utilitarian, rational look. According to sociologist Herbert Spencer, humans have developed empathy as an adaptation that has played an important survival role because it facilitates the impulse to help others. Humans have evolved as a very social species, so empathy is right at home in healthy human interactions. Empathy plays a constructive social role in the grand scheme of things and encourages socially beneficial behavior. On the individual level, this means helping out a neighbor or relative in need. On a higher level, it means people coming together to accomplish great feats of civilization.

The definition of empathy usually categorizes it into three main types: affective, somatic, and cognitive empathy. Affective empathy is about emotions, which people usually think about when discussing empathy. It's your ability to understand what someone else is feeling and emotionally react to that. For instance, when your partner's emotional state makes you worry about them, you are experiencing affective empathy. A more pronounced manifestation of this is when their emotional pain causes distress or outright pain for you, as well.

Somatic empathy is interesting because it involves spontaneous physical reactions to what someone else is experiencing. For example, when you witness embarrassment or emotional distress in another person and feel a physical reaction such as blushing, an elevated heart rate, sweating, or an uneasy feeling in your stomach, that's somatic empathy.

Cognitive empathy relates to thoughts and is perhaps the most rational of the three types. You can understand what someone else is thinking without asking but solely based on their situation. Part of this ability is thanks to your own experience and logic; however, it also involves the conscious effort of putting yourself in the other person's shoes and imagining yourself facing that same situation. It's a quick exercise in mental role reversal; for some people, it's partly intuitive.

A distinction should be made between empathy and sympathy. Sympathy is fairly synonymous with compassion, so it definitely bears a fair amount of resemblance to empathy. However, sympathy tends to be passive, stopping short of making a real effort to understand another person, which is the essence of empathy. Feeling bad for someone having a rough time doesn't take a lot of emotional or mental effort. Still, you need empathy to truly understand them and feel what they're feeling. Sympathy can be felt for any random stranger on the street, but your partner (in an intimate relationship) is the person to whom you're connected on a deeper level.

You can fairly accurately assess your level of empathy based on how other people treat you. If they often approach you for advice, consider you a good listener, and confide in you about their problems, you are very likely empathetic. This isn't necessarily something that you and the other person have to discuss. People will simply feel how you empathize and naturally gravitate toward you.

Your own actions and responses are also something you should analyze. On the emotional level, you should consider how you respond to tragic news, how easily you detect deception, and how much you truly care about the problems of others. Deeply empathetic people will sometimes struggle to say no and establish personal boundaries, which is one example of how empathy can go too far. So, you should be careful and considerate with a deeply empathetic partner in a relationship since they will need you to respect them and have their best interest at heart.

Problems and Obstacles

As wonderful as empathy is, it can wreak havoc in your life if it isn't restrained by reason and self-respect. Not keeping your empathy under control can exhaust you and make you feel like the weight of the world is crashing down on you. Being overwhelmed by too much empathy will wear anybody down and lead to exhaustion. People with this problem often feel drained after extensive social interaction, which is the least of the issues that can arise.

These feelings are referred to as empathy fatigue, which is tiresome and can lead to an empathy shutdown overall. Feelings of weakness, isolation, and lethargy are common symptoms, and they can have a severe impact on your social interactions. Think of it like any other system where overexertion leads to a crash. It's particularly dangerous when this happens with empathy because you might become unresponsive or even lose compassion for periods of time. This isn't good for anyone, especially you and people very close to you, such as your partner. To avoid being overwhelmed by empathy, you need to keep things in perspective and stay realistic, employing logic and reason to understand that you can't always help everyone and that emotionally draining yourself will have no positive effects on anyone, least of all yourself.

Empathy fatigue is one of the causes behind a lack of empathy, but it's usually periodic. There are many other reasons people might lack empathy in certain situations or life in general. A lack of empathy often results in antisocial behavior and has a profoundly negative effect on relationships. Significant personality disorders, such as narcissism, can accompany it. However, healthy individuals can also have diminished empathy.

A lack of empathy can result in antisocial behavior.
https://www.pexels.com/photo/photo-of-man-leaning-on-wooden-table-3132388/

Common barriers to empathy include cognitive biases, which come in various forms. Having a cognitive bias can make it difficult for you to interpret the world objectively. Having a hard time understanding other people and their feelings is just one of the symptoms of this thinking error. Cognitive biases can sometimes be rather subtle, making them tricky to eliminate. A common cognitive bias that diminishes empathy is the idea that people who go through a rough time can only blame themselves for their circumstances.

When you look at the world through such a lens, it's very hard to empathize with people and their predicaments. Internally, a cognitive bias can result from being too harsh on yourself, thus projecting the same scrutiny onto others. Suppose you have a very low opinion of yourself and always think that everything bad that happens to you is solely your own failure. In that case, you may very well treat the problems of others in the same way. The opposite can also be true since some people will lack compassion when looking at other people's failures while, at the same time, always attributing personal failures to external factors.

All sorts of preconceived notions, distractions, and inclinations toward judgment can also make empathy difficult. Victim blaming is a common problem that diminishes people's empathy. It's a very easy pit to fall into and can creep up on you in the subtlest and most unexpected of ways, as it's not always egregious and can even sound reasonable. Think about a hypothetical scenario involving a tragic traffic accident involving a pedestrian who was jaywalking.

Quite a few people will react to the news by commenting that the pedestrian shouldn't have been jaywalking and that they would still be alive had they obeyed traffic regulations. While this may be very true, it is a statement that serves no practical purpose other than suppressing empathy. The empathetic response would be to acknowledge the tragedy, wonder about the victim's family, or even offer assistance if possible.

The problem with victim blaming is that it can be strangely gratifying, which is why many people do it unconsciously and default to it. Commenting that someone could have avoided their negative outcome demonstrates perceived personal competence, noting that the commentator would have done better or been smarter in a given situation. These statements stroke the ego, but they don't really help anyone or offer any value, least of all to the person making the statement. As you can see, this attitude can easily apply to relationships and is, unfortunately, quite common.

In almost all cases, the antidote is to listen attentively and actively to what other people are telling you, especially your partner. Everything you've learned about empathizing and communicating in the previous sections will help you unblock your mind. Letting go of biases and breaking the habit of preconceptions and conclusion-jumping can sometimes be a significant mental undertaking, but there is a lot you can do to bolster your empathy.

Developing and Cultivating Empathy

Putting aside cases that involve severe mental health issues, deeply entrenched personality disorders, or brain damage, empathy is a skill that you can learn and improve a fair amount. In some ways, it's like a muscle group that you must train with the right exercises – if you want to strengthen it. The overwhelming majority of people can do this with empathy without much trouble. It's usually not difficult, especially when you're in a relationship, but it can sometimes take a while.

Apart from previously discussed methods like active listening, learning the ins and outs of body language can also help bolster your empathy. Reading body language boils down to taking note of your partner's posture, subtle facial expressions, and gestures. These are non-verbal cues that people give off mostly unconsciously, and they can reveal things like openness, comfort, discomfort, anxiety, relaxation, happiness, frustration, and countless other emotions and mental states.

A common worksheet used in individual and group therapy sessions with clients who struggle with empathy entails telling an empathy story. The first step is to choose a certain story, which can be a story about someone you know or something you've read in the paper. After choosing a story, you can choose the medium you want to use to tell it, like writing, video, narration, art, or anything else that applies. It can also be told in person, directly to someone else.

Your significant other would be the ideal partner for this exercise. The point of the exercise is to tell the story in a way that emphasizes how the protagonist felt and why, with an attempt to dissect and understand those emotions. Explain what that person felt and why, then do your best even if you don't find the story relatable. Using a relatable story would work best, but identifying one can be difficult when you struggle with a lack of empathy. Once you tell and analyze the story, you should ask your partner to analyze it similarly and describe the emotions they could identify. You and your partner can both choose and tell these stories, regardless of whether or not empathy is an issue for both of you. In fact, if one partner is more empathetic than the other, the other side could learn quite a lot from them during this exercise.

Something else you and your partner can do is the so-called "What Am I Feeling?" game. The premise is very simple, involving various topics that can be summarized in single words, which will serve as cues. The idea is to pick a topic and then try to guess what your partner is feeling or thinking about. This can be an especially effective exploratory activity for romantic partners because they usually know each other quite well. It can be an entirely verbal game, or you could make cards with different words or topics written on them.

In general, one of the quintessential mental tricks to stimulate your empathy is to train your brain to seek out similarities instead of differences in people. This is such a simple yet incredibly effective mental change that can help you see the world in a very different light if you manage to turn it into a habit. Your brain will spot all the minuscule ways you are different from someone else very easily and often by default.

This is natural, and it's not a problem in and of itself, but the trick is to remember not to make those differences the area of focus when perceiving someone else. Focusing instead on all the similarities you share with others whenever you're out and about will gradually make you more open to seeing who they are and what they are feeling. This is a fundamental change in the thinking process for many people, so there are many daily opportunities to practice it.

Whether the issue is with your partner or people in general, growing your empathy requires daily practice while avoiding the obstacles above. Listen instead of interrupting, ask well-intentioned questions instead of judging, and focus on people's feelings. It sounds simple enough, but it might require a prolonged commitment to get the hang of it. However, seeing as you've made it to a point in your life where you are in a serious relationship, becoming more empathetic is likely a matter of minor attitude adjustments and just talking more with your partner.

Section 9: Vulnerability – Strength through Openness

It should be clear by now that vulnerability in relationships has much to do with trust and intimacy, but it's also a quality of its own. Unfortunately, vulnerability carries a negative connotation in many people's minds, although the aversion is understandable. As emotional creatures prone to all sorts of insecurities and worries, human beings naturally fear being hurt emotionally. Self-preservation is an instinct that all living things possess, but humans are the only beings whose self-preservation instincts go well beyond just preserving physical integrity.

Vulnerability is a quality that disarms your partner and allows them to open up and trust you more.

Photo by Liza Summer: https://www.pexels.com/photo/woman-comforting-desperate-girlfriend-and-embracing-gently-6382530/

For people, emotional damage can be just as, if not more frightening than physical harm. As a consequence, emotional vulnerability in our modern society is discouraged and generally stigmatized, but the real trouble is when vulnerability is falsely equated with weakness. Nobody wants to be seen as weak, and that's completely natural. Still, the truth is that vulnerability doesn't imply weakness and that it has a vital role to play in relationships. This section will explore that idea in more depth and delve into how vulnerability can be encouraged, developed, and put to healthy use in your relationship.

Vulnerability in Relationships

In the context of romantic relationships, vulnerability primarily concerns your ability and readiness to open yourself up emotionally to your partner. As you've seen in previous discussions, opening up to your partner and having that openness reciprocated is half the battle. It's impossible to build trust with your partner without being open, and it's even less likely that you'll be able to strengthen emotional or even physical intimacy when you shut them out.

Vulnerability and trust are so closely intertwined because the decision to truly open yourself up to another person carries inherent risks – or at least perceived risks. It's somewhat of a chicken and egg dilemma, too, since allowing yourself to be vulnerable enables you to build up trust, while trust makes it easier to be vulnerable. These two crucial aspects of your relationship feed into each other, are strongly correlated, and must be nurtured equally.

Showing your true feelings and vulnerability also entails letting the other person in on your weaknesses, which everyone has. This is one of the reasons many people wrongfully treat vulnerability and weakness as synonymous. While showing your weaknesses to the entire world is not the most sustainable strategy, it works differently in intimate relationships. Your partner should know and be mindful of your weaknesses if they explain and understand where you're coming from and empathize with you more deeply.

Without understanding and empathy, relationships will never reach that deeper level and become as strong as you need them to be. This is how vulnerability becomes a source of strength. It initially strengthens the relationship by bringing a couple closer and developing their bond. Since being in a healthy relationship with someone who supports and understands you without judgment can change your entire life, vulnerability also strengthens the individual.

Think about all those personal problems that people might have, which they keep hidden and suppressed out of fear. More often than not, letting the right person in is exactly what's needed to tackle those problems and begin healing. Unaddressed, these issues will only worsen over the years, making functioning in relationships and life difficult. This is how misguided attempts to project an image of strength by closing yourself off from the world lead to real weakness.

The fear of judgment is why many people avoid being vulnerable. It's especially unfortunate when this fear is vindicated by opening up to the wrong person and getting hurt, which can certainly happen. If you've had an experience like that, it's understandable if you're reluctant to allow yourself to be vulnerable. Nonetheless, you should look at it through the prism of risk and reward, understanding that the reward of opening up to the right person is well worth the emotional risk.

One of the underappreciated benefits of vulnerability is that it can promote personal growth. It's not just about revealing your problems or weaknesses and allowing your partner to help you overcome them. Openness means letting another person in on all your hopes and dreams in life, even those you are insecure about because you might feel they are silly or unrealistic.

It's not uncommon for people to convince themselves that a certain goal or dream they have is unrealistic or even worthy of ridicule. Goals can certainly be objectively too lofty, but few things are impossible to accomplish with enough work, dedication, and motivation. Sometimes, the support and guidance of someone you trust might be just the boost you need to unlock your true potential.

The bottom line with vulnerability in relationships is that it's simply necessary. Without it, there can be no deeper understanding, no true empathy, and no way for your partner to see things from your perspective. This pitfall can ruin most relationships because feeling understood and truly known is one thing that draws people to relationships in the first place. Not being understood is a fairly common reason that people cite when explaining why their relationship feels emotionally unsatisfying or why it ended.

Some folks don't realize that being understood isn't something they should leave entirely to their partner and just expect it by default. It takes effort on both sides, which mostly boils down to opening up. You can consider this in a very practical sense, as well. In healthy relationships, partners will understand each other's needs, desires, expectations, and boundaries well. When people in a relationship aren't open with each other and constantly close off due to their inhibitions, it will be very difficult to communicate their expectations and outlook on the relationship overall.

These barriers will inevitably lead to conflict, dissatisfaction, unmet needs, disappointment, and much more detrimental to a relationship's prospects. If you need your partner to understand you and meet your expectations, you shouldn't make it more difficult for them. They can be the most empathetic person in the world, but if you hold on to your fear of letting them in and are continuously shutting them off, there will be little they can do to get through to you. Thus, working on your vulnerability or helping your partner work on theirs is sometimes the first step needed to strengthen your relationship.

Encouraging Vulnerability in Your Relationship

The first step toward making vulnerability less taboo is simply talking about it. A thorough discussion about the concept of vulnerability, how it might fit into your relationship, and what it means to you and your partner can be just the thing to get the ball rolling. Let your partner know how vulnerability makes you feel while also making sure they express their feelings about it.

You need to tell each other what the act of vulnerability makes you feel.

People who have an aversion toward vulnerability can react to it in different ways. Some will feel anxious, others will get moderately depressed, and some will react with anger. Furthermore, what people feel isn't always what they express clearly. When feeling vulnerable, your partner might visibly react by going quiet while, under the surface, they are experiencing intense anger. Whatever the case is with you or your partner, to be fully understood, these emotions must be discussed, as they might require different approaches.

Past experiences with vulnerability are also a valuable topic to explore. However, personal history can be one of the more difficult topics to take up. Suppose you or your partner can explain when and how you were hurt in the past, especially before your relationship. In that case, you might gain quality insight into ways to help each other feel more comfortable and trusting.

You must lead by example, especially if only one of you is struggling. It's not enough to tell your partner they should be more open and less fearful of vulnerability. No matter how well you frame it and how rational of a case you state for openness, you still have to practice what you preach. You should show your partner that neither of you should have anything to fear and that you feel perfectly comfortable sharing your thoughts, feelings, and fears with them. Ensure they can see how much they help you when they listen and understand your concerns. It will make them feel good to know that you are relying on them.

This is a strong motivator for them to reciprocate and start opening up more to you. It's about promoting a sense of security in your relationship and creating a space of safety and empathy. It's also not enough to simply trust your partner without accounting for why they might have trouble doing the same. You must always do your best to be trustworthy and reliable, not just by being honest but also by leaving no room for them to doubt you. Don't leave things unsaid and unaddressed because that's how you create room for their thoughts to feed on their insecurities.

Trust can be very fragile for people struggling with vulnerability, so you must start small and be careful. Even in the most mundane and seemingly unimportant situations, demonstrating your openness and trustworthiness can go a long way toward making your partner more relaxed. If you have to crawl before walking, so be it, but you're likely to be surprised by how fast you can create a more comfortable environment if you make the right adjustments. The most important thing in terms of trust is to ensure that your partner feels they can trust you with their feelings. The way toward that goal is through empathy, listening, and being open about your own issues.

Fostering Vulnerability in the Long Term

Vulnerability can be encouraged in your partner on a regular basis, and it doesn't necessarily have to be a single thing you need to change at some specific point. How comfortable a couple is with being vulnerable depends on how they carry themselves in their daily life, including subtle changes in behavior and communication. You can partake in certain exercises with your partner to strengthen this bond.

Avoiding the Pitfall of Judgment

As mentioned, judgment is one of the biggest obstacles to vulnerability and openness. While some people struggle with opening up, others struggle to be less judgmental. Just like the fear of weakness, judgment is a problem rooted in some natural human impulses. It has its role to play in other human affairs, but in relationships, what you think doesn't always have to be what you say. Open communication is paramount, but there are different ways to express certain opinions. To become less judgmental, the best thing you can do is learn how to truly listen.

If your partner opens up about something they've done wrong or a weakness they might have, your first thoughts might be negative and critical. You shouldn't be ashamed of these thoughts, but choosing how you're going to externalize your concerns is up to you. One previously mentioned aspect of active listening is especially important when encouraging vulnerability. That aspect is the art of asking open-ended questions. Whenever you see signs that your partner is slowly opening up about something, remember to encourage them by asking questions and formulating them in a way that provides the maximum possible space for them to keep talking.

Apart from employing active listening to encourage your partner to share, you can also choose when and where to address your partner's admissions. Sometimes, the best thing to do is to affirm them when they open up and then schedule a more thorough conversation on the topic later in the day. This will give you time to collect your thoughts and come up with ways to respond with a supportive, non-judgmental attitude.

Self-Reflection and Awareness

While it could be your partner who has a problem with vulnerability, you may also have to have a conversation with yourself. If you find that, time and time again, your partner shuts you out, avoids serious topics, and deflects from their emotions, ask yourself and your partner what you can do to make it easier for them.

Be empathetic and reverse your roles, at least in your mind. Imagine that you're the one who's sharing a deep fear, uncomfortable past experience, or any other troubling concern. Then, list ways you typically respond to your partner's moments of vulnerability, including verbal and non-verbal responses. Do your best to imagine how those responses would make you feel in your own moments of vulnerability. The central question should be whether or not those responses would encourage you to share more or to shut down the conversation. You should also ask your partner for their input regarding whether or not you're a good listener and which of your typical responses make them uncomfortable with sharing. Together, you can create a definitive list of behaviors and statements that make your partner feel judged.

The Importance of Gratitude

Gratitude is an excellent form of encouragement regarding vulnerability, although it's often overlooked. Take a moment to think about a stereotypical group therapy setting, such as support groups for substance abuse. You'll see the perfect example of how gratitude encourages sharing. These groups contribute to creating a non-judgmental space and are usually successful in opening up even the most stubborn participants.

Whenever a participant shares a troubling story, the therapist will explicitly thank them for sharing, and the entire group will validate them. This is easier to do in support groups because they are made up of people with similar experiences, but gratitude as a replacement for judgment is a simple concept that works well in all worldly situations. It could take some training, but you can get the hang of it fairly easily. Whenever your partner opens up about something, make it a habit to respond with something like, "Thanks for telling me," or, "I appreciate you telling me." When this becomes instinctual for you, it will eventually completely replace judgmental statements. How you communicate also affects your mind, so it's likely that it'll evolve past mere speech and gradually make you less judgmental on a fundamental level.

Daily Openness

Being open with your partner should be omnipresent throughout your days together. Vulnerability sometimes entails opening up about something big and very painful, but in most cases, it's found in those little things in life and how you interact daily. The main aspect is to be honest about your feelings regardless of the topic.

For instance, people might avoid admitting that their feelings have been hurt for many reasons. Sometimes, it's their fear of weakness, but there are also cases where people worry so much about their partner's feelings that they completely disregard their own. Telling someone they've hurt you in any way can be just as distressing to the offending party, especially when the offense was unintentional.

If you think about everything you've learned about communication and conflict resolution in this book, you'll remember there are healthy ways to address any concern. Whether your partner has caused you deep emotional pain or simply forgotten to buy the groceries you asked for, the approach is the same. All those minor infractions and annoyances that occur in every relationship are opportunities for you and your partner to practice openness.

Interpersonal Exploration

You should set aside some time weekly to discuss this aspect of your relationship with your partner. A comfortable and controlled setting can be much more conducive to honest expression than a discussion that comes out of the spur of the moment. For instance, discussing your fears with your partner is always beneficial.

Fears are very prone to exaggeration when suppressed and bottled up because your mind has ways of filling certain gaps on its own. Without support and understanding, which includes valuable advice and guidance from the people you trust, your mind will allow the fear to grow – and, eventually, take over. When you externalize it by writing it down on a list or naming different fears with your partner, your fear will likely feel smaller. The insights you get from your partner can also put the fear in perspective and allow you to examine it in a new, more rational light. Whether it's your fears or something else, exploration exercises with your partner will uncover many things you've kept bottled up. You'll often find that the problem only needed a set of fresh eyes, and the solution had been staring you in the face all along.

Section 10: Keeping the Spark Lit in the Long Term

When couples can work together and resolve their problems effectively, these relationships will enjoy a degree of long-term stability – enabling all the nice things in life to flourish.

Suppose you always fight and experience insecurity with your partner. In that case, finding room to enjoy things together will prove difficult. All those activities that happy couples engage in, often naturally and without much thought, are the spice of life that keeps relationships feeling fresh and exciting for a long time.

Keeping the spark in your relationship ongoing is always a work in progress.
https://www.pexels.com/photo/group-of-people-with-sparkling-bengal-lights-4997798/

Some couples need less excitement than others, as many people are perfectly happy spending quiet evenings with their significant other and only occasionally require that need for excitement. If it works, it's certainly not broken, but it's also true that people can sometimes neglect this part of the relationship. These oversights can make relationships less stimulating and fulfilling, producing all sorts of tension. Some people just put up with it and let things run their course, resigned to the idea that losing that spark is normal. It's one of the reasons a very common misconception exists that long-term relationships will inevitably become stale and uninteresting. In reality, rekindling the flame takes just a bit of effort and patience with one another. Nothing more.

The Wonders of Long-Term Partnership

The misconception that long-term relationships eventually lose their spark is all too common and very unfortunate. First and foremost, embracing this mentality can discourage some people from committing to serious relationships or marriage in the first place. However, it also sometimes manifests as an unwillingness to improve relationships in crisis. Some people will end up unhappy in their relationship and resign in apathy, allowing problems to accumulate and worsen because they believe it's just a natural course they can't change.

No matter how long a relationship has been going, there is no reason to accept the apparent loss of vigor and excitement. It's a tragic path because it results in you and your partner missing out on many great things in life. When it comes to marriage, the later years can really be the best time of the relationship if each spouse takes the right steps!

With continuous effort and perhaps some creativity, you and your partner can come up with new ways to keep the fire lit for many years. Effort doesn't necessarily imply hard work, as that's necessary only in relationships in a severe crisis. The effort to keep the spark going for a loving couple comes naturally and is simply made up of all those small but meaningful things you can do to make each other happy on a daily basis. It means activities and ideas you'll both enjoy, fulfilling your lives.

The emotional connection between two people who meet in the world and then decide to spend their lives together is something quite special in human relationships. People are inherently connected to their parents, siblings, and other close family members. As powerful and important as those connections are, they're almost always the default.

They're natural, presumed, and often taken for granted. Meeting someone along your journey and making a connection is a whole other ballgame.

It's a sad reality that some people won't have the same luck and will struggle to find someone to truly connect with, or they'll miss out on an opportunity because they fail to put in the effort. The important people you meet along the way have the potential to learn everything about you and understand you in a way that even most parents can't. Having that kind of support in your life is a priceless gift, and that's what makes long-term relationships worth the continuous effort over the years.

Such a support system can unlock a person's potential in ways they never imagined, not just regarding relationships but life overall. Many people walk around with passions, hopes, and dreams that lie dormant or have been suppressed due to a lack of motivation. Many people have had the experience of a sudden ambitious idea or plan for the future, only to rationalize and eventually abandon their ambitions. This is how complacency sets in and makes people averse to change and effort; this kind of lifeless behavior usually happens when you're alone.

When you have someone who truly knows you and has your best interest at heart, they will push back on your inertia and do their best to prevent you from becoming complacent. Whenever you come up with a reason not to pursue your goals, your significant other will be the person to offer a counterargument. They will poke holes in your excuses and remind you of your abilities that you might forget when you're on your own. Living without this support makes it easy to forget its power, but it's worth every effort to hold on to it once you have it.

Long-term healthy partnership also makes it easier to handle failures and defeats in life. Self-deprecation and discouragement will take hold much easier when you don't have someone to remind you to shift your perspective to the bigger image: that one failure is not the end of the world. A loving and true partner will bring out the best in you and constantly remind you of your strengths and virtues, making most failures look like temporary setbacks.

These are only some of how long-term relationships provide stability and serve as a source of motivation. Self-reliance is essential and can get you far in life, but a person can't go through life without stumbling somewhere along the way. That's where a support system with the one who loves you and whom you can trust comes in to make picking up the pieces easier.

Kindling for the Flame

Since maintaining the spark is a long-term endeavor involving a fair amount of creativity, it's a very open-ended goal. What a certain couple will do to keep things going over the years will depend on their individual traits, preferences, and much else. Every couple can and should strive to chart their own path and develop unique activities that they find stimulating. However, it needs to be said that whatever the choice is, compromise from both parties will yield the best results. The kindling that your relationship needs can include anything from hobbies to exciting adventures to how you communicate daily. Still, some ideas can be universally beneficial in most relationships.

Dating Doesn't Have to Stop

Just as you would do to strengthen intimacy, having regular date nights over the years is always a good way to keep a relationship dynamic and fresh. Whatever your age and however long you've been in your relationship or marriage, there is no point where going on dates together becomes outplayed or somehow unbecoming. If you've ever heard someone say something along those lines, you should certainly disregard these stigmas.

Going out to dinner or for a drink, especially in new and exciting places, will break up your boring routine in many ways. It's rarely about the drink or dinner there; it's really about going through something new and exciting with your loved one. It doesn't necessarily have to be the most exciting date in the world, as simply changing the scenery and doing old things in new settings can be enough to mix things up. Dates are open to infinite improvisations and creativity, though, so they can certainly be exciting as well if you and your partner are up for it.

The Power of Spontaneity

You should aim for spontaneity and novelty if things get a bit too familiar. For instance, there is a fine line between a midlife crisis and trying something you simply didn't have the time or money for when you were younger. Suppose there was ever a hobby you or your partner wanted to take up but didn't get around to for any reason. In that case, it might be a stimulating shared activity for the two of you.

Vacations are another great way to spice things up because they, just like hobbies and dates, allow much experimentation and novelty. Surprise vacations and dates can create very fulfilling experiences, but old things can also be tried in new and exciting ways for added variety. For instance, going on a biking trip to a place you used to visit only by car is a very stimulating outdoor activity. Surprises are always guaranteed to create excitement in relationships because intimate partners know each other very well, minimizing the possibility of unpleasant surprises. Plus, it's always nice to be remembered without prompting.

Trips Down Memory Lane

Making experiences out of revisiting dear old memories in your relationship is another activity that can have an incredibly positive effect on couples. This can mean revisiting a place of significance for a vacation, but it can also include various activities that you used to enjoy years ago. Sometimes, people will gradually stop doing the things they enjoy because they simply forget about them over time, distracted by the requirements of life.

Committing to creating memories together and revisiting them is a rejuvenating experience.
https://www.pexels.com/photo/man-and-woman-sitting-on-brown-wooden-table-4554383/

It can be a very rejuvenating experience to relive old moments, passions, places, and activities, especially when combined with spontaneity and surprises. Relational memory in the human mind can be strange in how it associates the things you remember with the things you feel. Taking a trip down memory lane can thus be much more than fun. It can uncover long-forgotten and buried feelings in ways you least expect. An old place or setting that has significance in your relationship's history can trigger a sudden wave of intense emotions that will be just as strong as they were the first time.

Intimacy

Intimacy is something you should continuously work on. Beyond improving your communication and strengthening your bond, it can also keep a relationship exciting. This is because many intimacy-building activities and exercises are stimulating and engaging. You should always try to share your fantasies, hopes, and dreams with your partner, even if they are new ones that didn't occur to you before.

Throughout the years ahead, never forget the importance of all those little moments of intimacy that consistently keep romantic partners close. Whether snuggling up on the couch to watch a movie, just holding hands, or any other kind of basic physical contact, happy couples will continue to do it even in old age. Not everyone expresses their affection in the same way, of course, but you and your partner should create and preserve your own unique language of intimacy and love.

Never Stop Communicating

The ideas for the things you can do to give your relationship the occasional boost are virtually endless. The main thing is to communicate effectively and consistently. Surprises can be great, but partners in a relationship should never be reluctant to voice their ideas for something new that they might be interested in. Conversely, they should not be afraid to voice their concerns or fears either. You can sit down in the evening and formulate a written, multi-year plan for an exciting future with your partner. Envision, in complete honesty, a list of things that both of you would like to do and experience just to bring more fulfillment into your life. Some of these things could be what you would have been unable to do without your partner's support and participation.

Couples who talk to each other with the same openness and willingness through the years are the ones with the best prospects. There is simply no way to deal with the challenges in your relationship if you don't harness the power of communicating with your partner. Without it, you'll never understand what's wrong, what you should do, or what will make both of you happier. When communication breaks down, relationships gradually fall apart or devolve into years of unacknowledged misery. So, remember to cherish trust with your partner and keep it safe from harm.

BRAVING

Every couple has their own story, which means each one will have their unique formula for long-term success in their relationship. Only you and your partner/spouse can do what needs to be done to live your lives in love and understanding for a long time. You should try to take the things you've learned in this book, adapt them, and apply them in the most optimal way to meet the specific requirements of your relationship. That can mean focusing on some areas more than others or crafting a unique toolset that works for you.

That being said, you've also seen that some things are universal in healthy relationships. There have been quite a few interesting strategies developed by psychologists, couple therapists, and other experts over time, which are worth exploring if you and your partner want to try something that's tried and true. Many of these methods go back to the 50 years of extensive work and research conducted by John Gottman and his wife, Dr. Julie Schwartz-Gottman. As mentioned earlier in this book, these methods focus on various aspects of human relationships, but they especially stress the importance of trust.

Brené Brown, a researcher and professor at the University of Houston, developed an interesting concept. She devised it as the acronym BRAVING, simplifying the meaning of trust by breaking it down into seven key qualities and behaviors. BRAVING aims to help people understand things they need to focus on to facilitate long-term trust. You should consider this concept as a method to build trust and sustain it over time. It applies to all manner of relationships, including the one with your partner.

In a way, the BRAVING concept summarizes many of the lessons you've learned in this book, and it's an excellent foundation to return to for reassured and lasting stability in your relationship. It consists of the following elements:

Boundaries – The element of boundaries refers to personal boundaries and personal space, but it also has to do with various other limits. Boundaries are all about moderation, patience, the ability to sometimes say no, and respecting your partner's occasional need to say no. You and your partner must clearly understand what each of you considers acceptable or unacceptable in the relationship. Practicing continuous respect for each other's person, individuality, and personal pursuits is essential to ensuring that your relationship remains a place of comfort and support, as opposed to an overbearing method of control.

Reliability – Reliability is one of the best ways to reinforce and maintain trust. Couples who know they can count on each other to honor agreements and plans will create an environment of consistency and stability. More than anything else, reliability means that you and your partner will consistently follow through on what you say and do over the years. Breaking ten promises in a row and fulfilling one won't offset the damage and make up for letting them down. The key to consistent reliability is understanding one's limits and realizing that keeping promises and ensuring you never overpromise is equally crucial.

Accountability – If you are to resolve conflicts and get to the root of the issues that arise over time, you and your partner both need to acknowledge your mistakes. However, admitting you did something wrong is only the first step. True accountability to your partner means admitting your mistakes while also making an honest effort to make amends and avoid said mistake again. On the flip side, accountability is something that has to be encouraged through patience and forgiveness. If you default to judgment, anger, and stonewalling out of spite, you won't allow your partner to make things right.

Vault – What Brené Brown calls "the vault" is a couple's ability to confide in each other with complete certainty that deeply personal information will remain within the relationship. This goes back to the fact that vulnerability is important in relationships but isn't necessarily a flag you want to fly in front of the whole world. When your partner tells you something sensitive, it should remain between you, as if locked in a vault. Keeping each other's secrets promotes trust and reliability. Consider how you'd perceive someone who constantly spreads gossip or reveals personal information about someone, even if they just met you. You would hardly consider that person trustworthy, and rightfully so.

Integrity – Integrity dramatically affects all your interactions with other people, especially important relationships. It's about doing the right thing even when it's uncomfortable and practicing what you preach. Everyone can declare a set of values they supposedly have, but if they don't embody these behaviors, their value system will hardly inspire respect and admiration. In a way, integrity is about being able to trust yourself and, in turn, building trust with someone else. Taking emotional shortcuts and avoiding necessary discussions just to maintain the illusion of comfort will be detrimental to your relationship in the long run. As Brown explains it, having integrity is putting courage before comfort.

Non-Judgment – Judgment discourages trust and vulnerability and can be the end of relationships faster than you might expect. As you've seen in previous sections, learning to let go of your instinct to judge is essential in relationships because it clears the way for many things that make relationships great, such as understanding, openness, trust, safety, empathy, communication, and much more. You should also not forget the pitfall of self-judgment. If you're too hard on yourself, it can be more difficult to ask for help and open up to your partner. This can cause as much damage as being judgmental toward your partner.

Generosity – In BRAVING, generosity has a lot to do with giving the benefit of the doubt to your partner and how you interpret intent. It's about assuming that they didn't mean to hurt you, to give them the opportunity and encouragement to clear the air and make amends. If they forget your birthday, for instance, the generous thing is to assume that they had a lot going on that day, were busy, or were going through some problems. This opens the way for a constructive conversation instead of getting angry and focusing exclusively on how your partner's failure affects you personally.

Conclusion

As long as you and your partner or spouse love each other and feel that your relationship is worth preserving, there is always hope to solve any problem that comes your way. Remember that all human beings are fallible creatures. Poor decisions will sometimes be made, issues will arise, and life will throw some curveballs your way. It's not uncommon for relationships to start going through turbulence due to the common hardships of life.

Whatever the case in your relationship, the simple truth is that only you and your partner can help yourselves by deciding that you want to fix things. The fact that you've read this book and are looking for solutions demonstrates your commitment to this relationship, which is a great first step. Suppose you do decide that you need professional help. In that case, that's also an entirely valid path to take toward saving your relationship. However, even that will require some engagement with your partner, as you first need to agree to take that step.

The things you've learned in this book should help you in two main ways. First, this information should encourage you to reflect on things and analyze your relationship objectively to identify where the problems reside. Second, you should now know how to address some of those problems.

Once you get a foot in the door and start engaging with your partner the right way, there might be a very positive snowball effect. These efforts will likely be reciprocated when you take steps to get closer to your partner and open up to them. This is especially true if you're engaging with your partner while reading this book, which is the best way to go about it. The more input you seek from your partner, the easier it will get to share ideas and reach compromises.

After all, it's not up to only you to fix your relationship: It's up to both of you to get your entire toolkits together and give it your best shot as a team. At the end of the day, that's what relationships are all about, and if two people can come together to take on the challenges of life itself, then they doubtlessly also have the power to join forces to preserve what they've built.

If you enjoyed this book, I'd greatly appreciate a review on Amazon because it helps me to create more books that people want. It would mean a lot to hear from you.

To leave a review:

1. Open your camera app.
2. Point your mobile device at the QR code.
3. The review page will appear in your web browser.

Thanks for your support!

Check out another book in the series

Infidelity Recovery

A Comprehensive Workbook for
Healing, Rebuilding Trust, and Restoring
Intimacy in Your Relationship

Emma Lancaster

References

Bailey, M. (2017, September 19). Why Two Is Better Than One: How to Do Goal Planning as a Couple. Www.linkedin.com. https://www.linkedin.com/pulse/why-two-better-than-one-how-do-goal-planning-couple-michele-bailey

Bickham, S. (2023, September 4). 10 Types of Intimacy in a Relationship. Choosing Therapy. https://www.choosingtherapy.com/types-of-intimacy/

Bisignano, A. (2017, September 25). 7 Ways to Practice Social Media Etiquette in Your Relationship. GoodTherapy.org Therapy Blog. https://www.goodtherapy.org/blog/7-ways-to-practice-social-media-etiquette-in-your-relationship-0925174

Carpenter, D. (2020, February 14). 3 Ways to Build Real Empathy for Others in Your Life. Verywell Mind. https://www.verywellmind.com/how-to-develop-empathy-in-relationships-1717547

Cherry, K. (2022, January 18). Why You May Have Trust Issues and How to Overcome Them. Verywell Mind. https://www.verywellmind.com/why-you-may-have-trust-issues-and-how-to-overcome-them-5215390

Cherry, K. (2023, February 22). What Is Empathy? Verywell Mind. https://www.verywellmind.com/what-is-empathy-2795562

Dodgson, L. (2018, October 24). 11 Signs Your Old Relationships are Affecting Your Current One. Business Insider. https://www.businessinsider.com/signs-your-old-relationships-are-affecting-your-current-one-2018-6

Eisenberg, S. (n.d.). Gottman Communication Assessment. Counseling | Therapy. https://www.thecenterforgrowth.com/tips/gottman-communication-assessment

Gillihan, S. J. (2023, April 4). 12 Signs a Past Trauma May Be Affecting Your Relationship |Psychology Today. Www.psychologytoday.com. https://www.psychologytoday.com/us/blog/think-act-be/202304/12-signs-a-past-trauma-may-be-affecting-your-relationship

Gould, W. R. (2023, March 7). Why Vulnerability in Relationships Is So Important. Verywell Mind. https://www.verywellmind.com/why-vulnerability-in-relationships-is-so-important-5193728

Gulotta, J. (2022, September 26). How to Build Trust in a Relationship: 22 Tips. Choosing Therapy. https://www.choosingtherapy.com/build-trust-relationship/

Hecker, D. (2014, February 13). Relationship Success: Balancing Togetherness and Individuality. HuffPost. https://www.huffpost.com/entry/relationship-success-bala_b_4776478

Jenner, N. (2023, March 22). The Concept of Individuality in a Relationship and Why It Is Essential. The Online Therapist. https://theonlinetherapist.blog/the-concept-of-individuality-in-a-relationship-and-why-it-is-essential/

Leigh, M. (2018, January 10). Setting Goals with Your Spouse + Printable Worksheet. Live Well Play Together. https://www.livewellplaytogether.com/setting-goals-with-your-spouse-2/

Lewandowski, G. W. (2021, June 10). The 10 Most Common Sources of Conflict in Relationships | Psychology Today. Www.psychologytoday.com. https://www.psychologytoday.com/us/blog/the-psychology-relationships/202106/the-10-most-common-sources-conflict-in-relationships

Loggins, B. (2021, September 27). Intimacy in Relationships: What It Is and How to Cultivate It. Verywell Mind. https://www.verywellmind.com/what-is-intimacy-in-a-relationship-5199766

Lopez, D., Baker, N., & Nenn, K. (2015). Gestalt Therapy: The Empty Chair Technique – Mental Health Recovery. Mentalhelp.net. https://www.mentalhelp.net/blogs/gestalt-therapy-the-empty-chair-technique/

Luna, K. (2018, August 9). It's Complicated: Our Relationship With Texting. https://www.apa.org/ . https://www.apa.org/news/press/releases/2018/08/relationship-texting

Mosemann, C. W. (2022, February 8). 5 Signs of Healthy Communication in a Relationship. Tidewater Physicians Multispecialty Group. https://www.mytpmg.com/5-signs-of-healthy-communication-in-a-relationship/

Narum, A. (n.d.). How to Plan for the Future in a Relationship | Remainly. Www.remainly.com. https://www.remainly.com/articles/how-plan-future-relationship

Ningthoujam, N. (2023, September 17). 6 Red Flags That Your Past Is Affecting Your Present Love Life. Healthshots. https://www.healthshots.com/mind/emotional-health/past-relationship-affecting-current-relationship/

Pace, K. (2016). Trust Is One of the Most Important Aspects of Relationships. MSU Extension. https://www.canr.msu.edu/news/trust_is_one_of_the_most_important_aspects_of_relationships

Pace, R. (2020, March 17). 15 Reasons for Lack of Trust in a Relationship. Marriage Advice - Expert Marriage Tips & Advice. https://www.marriage.com/advice/relationship/lack-of-trust-in-a-relationship/

Pace, R. (2021, November 29). 5 Types of Conflict in Relationships and How to Deal With Them. Marriage Advice - Expert Marriage Tips & Advice. https://www.marriage.com/advice/relationship/types-of-conflict/

Relationships and Communication - Better Health Channel. (2022, February 24). Www.betterhealth.vic.gov.au. https://www.betterhealth.vic.gov.au/health/healthyliving/relationships-and-communication#importance-of-communication

Rusnak, K. (2022, April 4). Quiz: What Is Your Relationship Communication Style? | Psychology Today. Www.psychologytoday.com. https://www.psychologytoday.com/us/blog/happy-healthy-relationships/202204/quiz-what-is-your-relationship-communication-style

Rusnak, K. (2022, March 9). The Importance of Vulnerability in Healthy Relationships | Psychology Today. Www.psychologytoday.com. https://www.psychologytoday.com/us/blog/happy-healthy-relationships/202203/the-importance-vulnerability-in-healthy-relationships

Scott, E. (2022, January 25). How to Improve Your Relationships With Effective Communication Skills. Verywell Mind; Verywell Mind. https://www.verywellmind.com/managing-conflict-in-relationships-communication-tips-3144967

Smith, S. (2015, May 25). Top 5 Most Common Reasons Why Couples Stop Having Sex. Marriage Advice - Expert Marriage Tips & Advice. https://www.marriage.com/advice/intimacy/5-reasons-why-theres-intimacy-missing-in-your-marriage/

Smith, S. (2022, January 31). 15 Relationship Conflict Patterns & Common Causes. Marriage Advice - Expert Marriage Tips & Advice. https://www.marriage.com/advice/relationship/conflict-in-relationships/

Smyth, T. (2019, April 16). Common Conflicts and Red Flags for Couples - Living With Finesse. Living with Finesse. https://livingwithfinesse.com/relationship-red-flags/

Start Here: 7 Evidence-Based Approaches to Improve Your Relationship. (2021, August 26). Psych Central. https://psychcentral.com/lib/simple-steps-to-improve-your-relationship#summary

Stevens, P. (2015, February 24). 10 Barriers To Intimacy and How You Can Break Them. The Warming Tree. https://thewarmingtree.wordpress.com/2015/02/24/10-barriers-to-intimacy-and-how-you-can-break-them/

Vakos, A. (2022, February 28). How To Deal With Unresolved Issues In A Relationship: 16 Effective Tips. A Conscious Rethink. https://www.aconsciousrethink.com/18439/unresolved-issues-in-a-relationship/

What Are The Effects Of A Lack Of Intimacy In A Relationship? | TAC. (2022, August 12). The Awareness Center. https://theawarenesscentre.com/what-are-the-effects-of-a-lack-of-intimacy-in-a-relationship/

Whitney-Coulter, A. (2021, February 5). Brené Brown on What it Really Means to Trust. Mindful. https://www.mindful.org/brene-brown-on-what-it-really-means-to-trust/

Williams, R. (n.d.). 6 Steps for Repairing Trust Issues from a Couples Therapist. IE Couples Counseling. https://www.iecouplescounseling.com/blog/how-to-deal-with-trust-issues-and-insecurities

Printed in Great Britain
by Amazon

46491390R10066